THE Singapore COOKBOOK

THE Singapore COOKBOOK

Over 200 tantalizing recipes

PUBLISHED BY

SALAMANDER BOOKS LIMITED

LONDON

A Salamander Book

Published by Salamander Books Limited
8 Blenheim Court
Brewery Road
London N7 9NT

ISBN 1 84065 110 5

1 2 3 4 5 6 7 8 9 10

All correspondence concerning the content of this volume should be addressed to Salamander Books Ltd.

Project managed by Charlotte Davies
Editorial Consultant Hilaire Walden
Editorial Assistant William M. Gilpin
Recipes by Kathryn Hawkins, Deh-Ta Hsiung, Lesley Mackley, Jasper Spencer-Smith, Hilaire Walden, Elizabeth Wolf-Cohen
Photography by Raymond Bragg, Simon Butcher, Ken Field, David Gill

Filmset SX Composing, England
Printed in Spain

When making any of the recipes in this book, you should follow either the metric or Imperial measures, as these are not interchangeable.

CONTENTS

SINGAPORE, the island republic lying off the southern tip of the Malaysian peninsular, is the smallest Asian state, but the population is one of the most richly varied, combining peoples of diverse cultures, races and religions, mainly Chinese, Malaysian and Indian. These multiracial, multicultural influences are reflected in Singaporean cuisine with intriguing effects. The fusion of ingredients, preparation techniques and cooking methods and styles make an appealing combination that exemplifies the character of the people as well as the food.

In general, Singaporean cuisine combines exuberance with a wonderful and subtle spiciness and sweetness that exudes enticing aromas. Many of the dishes are at once recognizeable yet with a character that is uniquely Singaporean.

Singaporean Chinese cooking is typical of the southern Cantonese and Hokkein style, with delicate flavours, clear sauces and much use of chicken, seafood and vegetables, but the addition of chillies, shrimp paste and tamarind give it a unique local taste.

The Malay influence (which itself combines aspects of Chinese, Indian and indigenous Malaysian cuisines) sees the greater use of fragrant spices and chillies, and the addition of coconut milk in both sweet and savoury recipes, curried-type dishes and satays.

Tamils from southern India have been responsible for the introduction of spiced, and often fiery, curry-type recipes, and tasty snacks such as curry puffs. As most Tamils are Hindus, and the climate of the country is too hot for the rearing of livestock for consumption, many of the Tamil dishes are vegetarian.

Singapore also has its own local speciality, Nonya cooking. In the 1820s many thousands of Chinese peasant labourers flocked across the Straits of Malacca from the rural districts of Swatow, Hainan and Hokkein to work on the construction of Singapore city. They took few women with them and so married the indigenous Malay Muslim population. The unique hybrid culture that developed is known as Peranakan or Straits Chinese, and its food is known as Nonya, after the women who cook it. Nonya cooking combines the original peasant Chinese ingredients and dishes with spicy Malay food, and takes advantage of the local herbs and seasonings such as galangal, turmeric, pandan leaves, limes, ginger, tamarind and chillies. Most dishes are cooked in a Chinese-style wok.

In Singapore, as in most Asian countries, a great deal of rice is eaten, and it is accompanies many dishes. A variety of different types of noodles are also popular as well as a meal accompaniment.

The local Chinese population eat their main meals in the traditional manner, with chopsticks and bowl, while Malaysian-influenced meals, such as a selection of curries, a sambal, and rice may be eaten with the fingers from improvised plates made from pieces of banana leaf.

Traditionally, eating is a communal affair and all the dishes for a meal are served at once, with everyone helping themselves.

However, Singaporean food is very adaptable and it can be divided into Western-style courses without any difficulty. Many of the recipes can also be served as snacks or simple one-dish (often one-pot) meals. In Singapore, many religions are practised – Hindu, Buddhism, Taoism, Islam and Christianity – and cultural events are celebrated so there are innumerable excuses to serve and enjoy fine, elaborate dishes that festive meals demand.

KEY INGREDIENTS

Bamboo shoots: Young tender shoots from the base of the bamboo shoots, these are crunchy but bland, absorbing stronger flavours. Sold canned.

Banana leaves: Used to make containers for steamed foods, to which they impart a delicate flavour.

Bean curd: Known as tofu in Japanese, this is a nutritious low-calorie food made from soy beans. Bland, with a soft-cheese texture, it absorbs other flavours. Stir-fry with care as it can disintegrate. 'Silken tofu' has a much softer texture and is mostly used in soups and sauces.

Bean sprouts: These small, young tender shoots are usually mung beans that have germinated, although other beans can also be allowed to sprout. Bean sprouts are nutritious, containing generous amounts of vitamins and minerals, and add a delicious crunch to stir-fry dishes.

Black beans: These small, fermented soy beans are very salty. Black bean sauce, in cans or bottles, is a quick, handy substitute.

Bok choy: Also known as Chinese cabbage, this resembles Swiss chard.

Celery cabbage (wong ah bok): A delicate pale green vegetable with a sweet taste that makes it ideal for use in salads. Its delicate flavour blends superbly with other foods.

Chillies: Add flavour as well as 'hotness'. Thais favour small and very fiery 'bird's eye' chillies but elsewhere these are only available in specialist shops. Chillies are rarely labelled with the variety or an indication of 'hotness'; as a rule of thumb, smaller varieties are hotter than large ones. Dried chillies have a more earthy, fruity flavour. The seeds and white veins inside a chilli are not only hotter than the flesh, but have less flavour, and are generally removed before using. Chillies contain an oil that can make the eyes and even the skin sting, so wash your hands after preparing them and avoid touching the eyes or mouth.

Chinese beans: The tender pods of these green beans can be eaten whole. Snap beans or French beans can be substituted.

Chinese black mushrooms: These dried mushrooms have quite a pronounced flavour and must be soaked fro 20-30 minutes before use. The stalks tend to be tough so are usually discarded. Available in Oriental food stores.

Chinese black vinegar: Black vinegars are made from grains other than rice, and aged to impart complex, smoky flavours with a light, pleasant bitterness. Substitute sherry, balsamic vinegar or a good red wine vinegar.

Choy dum (Chinese flowering cabbage): Very similar to 'bok choy' though slightly smaller, with narrower stalks and slightly paler leaves; the distinctive feature is the yellow flowers. These are cooked with the rest of the vegetable.

Coconut cream: The layer that forms on the top of coconut milk.

Coconut milk: Not the liquid from inside a coconut, but extracted from shredded coconut flesh that has been soaked in water. Soak the shredded flesh of 1 medium coconut in 315 ml (10 fl oz/1^1/$_4$ cups) boiling water for 30 minutes. Tip into a sieve lined with muslin or fine cotton and squeeze the cloth hard to extract as much liquid as possible. Coconut milk can also be made from unsweetened desiccated (shredded) coconut soaked in boiling water, or milk, which will be richer. Allow 315 ml (10 fl oz/1^1/$_4$ cups) liquid to 225 g (8oz/2^2/$_3$ cups) desiccated (shredded) coconut. Put into a blender and mix for 1 minute. Refrigerate coconut milk.

Coriander (cilantro) leaves: Best bought in large bunches rather than small packets. Stand bunches in cold water in a cool place.

Coriander (cilantro) roots: Roots have a more muted taste than the leaves. Large coriander bunches sold in Middle Eastern stores often include the roots. Fresh roots will last for several days if kept wrapped in a cool place, or can be frozen. If unavailable, use coriander (cilantro) stalks.

Daikon: A long, white, bland root vegetable with a crunchy texture, also called mooli or Japanese white radish.

Fish sauce: Also called nuoc nam and nam pla, this is made from salted, fermented anchovies and used in sauces, stir-fries and as a condiment. It is rich in protein and B vitamins and is salty, but the flavour is mild. The lighter Vietnamese and Thai sauces are best. A little goes a long way.

Five-spice powder: A blend of cinnamon, cloves, star anise, fennel and Szechuan pepper, used in Chinese marinades and sauces.

Galangal: Also known as Thai ginger, laos and lengk haus. There are two varieties, lesser and greater; the latter is preferred and more likely to be found in the West. It looks similar to root ginger but the skin is thinner, paler, more translucent and tinged with pink. Its flavour is also similar to ginger but less hot and with definite seductive citrus, pine notes. To use, peel and thinly slice or chop. The whole root will keep for up to 2 weeks if wrapped in paper and kept in the cool drawer of the refrigerator, or it can be frozen. Allow to thaw just sufficiently to enable the amount required to be sliced off, then return the root to the freezer. Galangal is also sold dried as a powder or in slices, the latter giving the better flavour. Substitute 1 dried slice or 1 teaspoon powder to each 1 cm (^{1}/$_4$in) used in a recipe; in recipes where fresh galangal is pounded with other spices, mix the dried form in after the pounding; elsewhere, use as normal.

Ginger root: This knobbly root's sweet spicy flavour is used in oriental soups, stir-fries and in fish dishes. Choose firm, heavy pieces that have a slight sheen. Store in a dark place, but do not refrigerate, for up to a week.

Gingko nuts: These have a hard shell, which must be removed before cooking, and a creamy coloured flesh. Shelled gingko nuts are also available in cans. If unavailable, substitute almonds.

Hoisin sauce: A reddish brown sauce based on soy beans and flavoured with garlic, chillies and a combination of spices. Flavours vary between brands, but it is nearly always quite sweet and it can range from the thickness of a soft jam to a runny sauce. It is used in Chinese marinades, barbecue sauces and stir-fries.

Kaffir lime leaves: The smooth, dark green leaves give an aromatic, clean citrus-pine flavour and smell. They keep well in a cool place and can be frozen. Use ordinary lime peel if kaffir lime leaves are unavailable, substituting 1^1/$_2$ teaspoons finely grated peel for 1 kaffir lime leaf.

Lemon grass: A long, slim bulb with a lemon flavour. To use, bruise the stems, cut off the root tip, peel the tough outer layers and cut away the top part of stalk. The stalks will keep for several days in a cool place, or they can be chopped and frozen. If unavailable, use the grated rind of ^{1}/$_2$ lemon or a lime in place of 1 stalk.

Long beans: Although these can grow to over 1 metre (3 feet) it is best to use younger ones. Green beans or French beans can replace them.

Lychees: Canned lychees are easy to find in supermarkets, but fresh ones are now becoming far more readily available. They need no more preparation than using the fingers to easily crack the knobbly, brittle coating. Beneath it, delicious white flesh surrounds a smooth central stone.

Mango: There are many different types of mango, each one varying in size, shape and colour. Select fruit that feels heavy for its size and is free of bruises or damage. A ripe mango yields to gentle pressure and should have an enticing, scented aroma. The flesh inside should have a wonderful, luxurious and slightly exotic texture and flavour but poor quality fruit can be disappointing; the key is the fragrance. If a mango is a little firm when bought, leave it in a warm sunny place to finish ripening.

Mushrooms: Chinese cooks seldom buy fresh mushrooms, preferring to use dried ones. These must be soaked before cooking. Put the mushrooms into a bowl, cover with boiling water, cover the bowl, leave for about 20-30 minutes until swollen and pliable, then drain well. If the stems are tough, discard them.
Cloud ear: Also known as 'wood ear', these are added for their texture rather than flavour, as they have little.
Straw: These thin, tall, leaf-like mushrooms are also known as 'paddy straw' or 'grass' mushrooms. They are sold canned as well as dried.
Winter black mushrooms: With a fairly intense, fragrant flavour, these are the most widely used.

Noodles: Most types are interchangeable, but two, rice stick noodles and bean thread noodles, can be crisp-fried. Dried noodles are usually soaked in cold water for 10-20 minutes until softened, before cooking; in general the weight will have doubled after soaking. After draining, the cooking will usually be brief.
Bean thread: Also called cellophane, mung bean, glass or shining noodles, these transparent noodles are made from ground mung beans. Stir into soups or stir-fry with vegetables. Soak in warm water for 5 minutes for general use, but use unsoaked in deep-frying.
Dried Chinese spaghetti: This thin firm noodle cooks quickly. Any thin spaghetti-type noodle can be used as a substitute. Chinese egg noodles are also widely available fresh in supermarkets and Asian markets.
Fresh rice noodles: Packaged cooked and wet in wide, pliable 'hanks'. To use, without unwinding, cut into ribbons and stir into a dish to warm through.
Rice sticks: Long, thin dried noodles made from rice flour, rice sticks (also known as rice vermicelli) can be fried directly in hot oils and increase many times in volume. A good base for any Chinese-style dish.

Oriental aubergine: These long, thin aubergines are tastier than the large ones, do not need peeling and do not absorb much oil. Sold in supermarkets and Asian markets.

Oyster sauce: A thick, brown, bottled sauce with a rich, subtle flavour, made from concentrated oysters and soy sauce. Often used in beef and vegetable stir-fry dishes.

Palm sugar: Brown sugar with a slight caramelized flavour, sold in cakes. If unavailable, use granulated sugar and demerera sugar in equal proportions.

Pandanus (screwpine): Both the leaves and the distilled essence of the flowers, called kewra water or essence, are used to give an exotic, musky, grassy flavour to Thai sweet dishes.

Pea aubergine: Very small aubergines about the size of a pea, and usually the same colour, although they can be white, purple or yellow. The fresh, slightly bitter taste is used raw in hot sauces and cooked in curries.

Pickled and preserved vegetables: Various types of vegetables, preserved, or pickled, in salt, are available in cans and plastic pouches, but if a label simply specifies 'Preserved Vegetable', it will invariably mean mustard greens. 'Turnip' is not the Western variety, but a type of radish.

Plum sauce: A thick, sweet Cantonese condiment made from plums, apricots, garlic, chillies, sugar, vinegar and flavourings. Use as a dip or a base for barbecue sauces.

Rice: Thais mainly use a good quality variety of long-grain white rice called 'fragrant' rice. Ordinary long-grain white rice can be substituted. To cook, rinse the rice several times in cold running water. Put the rice into a heavy saucepan with 315 ml (10 fl oz/1 1/4 cups) water, cover and bring quickly to the boil. Uncover and stir vigorously until the water has evaporated. Reduce the heat to very low, cover the pan tightly with foil, then place on the lid. Steam for 20 minutes until the rice is tender, light, fluffy and every grain is separate.
'Sticky' or 'glutinous' rice: An aptly named short, round grain variety. It can be formed into balls and eaten with fingers, or used for desserts.
Ground brown rice: Sometimes added to dishes to give extra texture. For this, dry-fry raw long-grain white rice until well-browned, then grind finely.

Rice vinegar: The mildest of all vinegars, with a sweet, delicate flavour and available in several varieties. If possible, use a pale rice vinegar for light-coloured sweet-and-sour dishes, and try a dark variety for dipping sauces. If neither is available, use cider vinegar. Use Japanese rice vinegar for salad dressings, sauces, and pickling; Chinese vinegar is not strong enough.

Rice wine: Made from fermented rice and yeast, this mellow wine is widely used for stir-fry cooking. Similar to sherry in colour, bouquet and alcohol content (18%), but with its own distinctive flavour. If unavailable, substitute a good dry sherry.

Rose wine: Imparts an exotic quality to foods. Use sweet sherry as a substitute.

Sesame oil: Made from toasted sesame seeds, this has a rich, golden brown colour and a nutty flavour and aroma. Has a low smoking point and can burn easily. As a seasoning, a teaspoon added to a stir-fry dish just before serving adds a delicious flavour.

Sesame seeds: Widely available, these add texture and flavour to stir-fry dishes. Dry-fry in the wok first to bring out flavour, then stir-fry and use as a garnish. Black sesame seeds can be interchanged with white ones – dry-fry them in the same way.

Shallots: Thai red shallots are smaller than Western ones. They have quite a pronounced flavour that is almost fruity rather than pungent. Ordinary shallots can be substituted.

Shrimps, dried: Whole dried shrimps are used to add texture and flavour.

Shrimp paste: A pungent, salty paste that is packed in jars, cans and plastic packets. Keep in a cool place.

Soy sauces: This essential Chinese condiment, flavouring and dipping sauce is made from a fermented mixture of soy beans, flour and water. The more delicate light soy sauce is most common. It is salty, but can be diluted with water. Dark soy sauce is thicker and sweeter, containing molasses or caramel. Japanese soy sauce, shoyu, is always naturally fermented.

Spring roll skins: These paper-thin flour-dough skins are sold as Shanghai wrappers or lumpia skins. They are thinner and fry more crisply than thicker Cantonese egg roll skins. They can be refrozen.

Star anise: This eight-pointed star-shaped pod has a mild liquorice flavour and is used in marinades.

Star fruit: Star fruit, also known as carambola, are long, almost translucent yellow, ridged fruit. The whole fruit is edible, and when cut across the width, the slices resemble five-pointed stars. Raw star fruit have a pleasant, citrus-like, juicy sharpness, but when poached the flavour is more distinctive.

Szechuan peppercorns: These aromatic, reddish brown dried berries have a mildly spicy flavour. Toast in a dry wok or frying pan before grinding to a powder.

Tamarind: Sold in sticky brown-black blocks, tamarind provides a sharp, slightly fruit taste. To make tamarind water, break off a 25 g (1 oz) piece, pour over 315 ml (10 fl oz/1¼ cups) boiling water. Break up the lump with a spoon, then leave for about 30 minutes, stirring occasionally. Strain off the tamarind water, pressing on the pulp. Discard the remaining debris and keep the water in a jar in the refrigerator. Ready-to-use tamarind syrup can sometimes be bought; it is usually more concentrated, so less is required.

Thai basil: Also called 'holy basil'. Thai basil leaves are darker and their flavour slightly deeper, less 'fresh', than ordinary sweet basil. Bundles of leaves can be frozen whole in a polythene bag for up to about 2 weeks; remove leaves as required and add straight to dishes. Substitute Thai sweet basil or ordinary sweet basil, if necessary.

Thai mint: This has a sweet flavour. If unavailable, Western spearmint or garden mint are the best substitutes.

Water chestnuts: A starchy, bland, crunchy tuber. Use raw in salads, or add to soups and stir-fries. Widely sold in cans; rinse in cold water, or drop briefly into boiling water then rinse, to remove any metallic taste.

Wonton skins: These smooth, wheat-flour dough wrappers about 7.5 cm (3 in) square are sold fresh and frozen in supermarkets and Asian markets.

Yellow bean paste/sauce: This thick, aromatic, spicy sauce is made from fermented yellow beans, flour and salt. It is used to flavour fish, poultry and vegetables.

SOUPS, STARTERS & SNACKS

SINGAPOREAN CHICKEN STOCK

1-1.25 kg (2¼-2¾ lb) chicken, giblets removed
2 slices fresh root ginger
1 clove garlic
2 spring onions (scallions)
large pinch of salt
large pinch of ground white pepper

Skin the chicken and trim away any visible fat. Wash and place in a large saucepan with remaining ingredients and 2 litres (70 fl oz/ 9 cups) of cold water.

Bring to the boil, skimming away surface scum using a large flat ladle. Reduce heat, cover and simmer gently for 2 hours. Allow to cool.

Line a sieve (strainer) with clean muslin (cheesecloth) and place over a large bowl. Ladle stock through sieve (strainer) and discard chicken and vegetables. Cover and chill. Skim away any fat that forms on the surface before using. Store in refrigerator for up to 3 days or freeze for up to 3 months.

Makes 1.75 litres (62 fl oz/7¾ cups).

SINGAPOREAN BEEF STOCK

900 g (2 lb) lean stewing beef
2.5 cm (1 in) piece fresh root ginger
1 clove garlic
2 shallots
1 stick celery
2 carrots
2 tablespoons dark soy sauce
large pinch of salt
large pinch of freshly ground black pepper

Trim any visible fat and silver skin from beef. Cut into 5 cm (2 in) pieces. Wash and pat dry with kitchen paper.

Place the beef in a large saucepan with the remaining ingredients and 2 litres (70 fl oz/ 9 cups) of cold water. Bring to the boil, skimming away surface scum using a large, flat ladle. Reduce heat, cover and simmer gently for 2 hours. Allow to cool.

Line a sieve (strainer) with clean muslin (cheesecloth) and place over a large bowl. Ladle stock through sieve (strainer) and discard beef and vegetables. Cover and chill. Skim away any fat that forms on the surface before using. Store in refrigerator for up to 3 days or freeze for up to 3 months.

Makes 1.85 litres (65 fl oz/8¼ cups).

SINGAPOREAN VEGETABLE STOCK

1 stalk lemon grass
2 slices fresh root ginger
1 clove garlic
2 spring onions (scallions)
115 g (4 oz) carrots, sliced
2 sticks celery
115 g (4 oz) bean sprouts
large pinch of salt
large pinch of ground white pepper

Break the lemon grass to release its flavour and place in a large saucepan with 2 litres (70 fl oz/9 cups) of cold water and all of the remaining ingredients.

Bring to the boil, skimming away surface scum using a large, flat ladle. Reduce heat, cover and simmer gently for 45 minutes. Allow to cool.

Line a sieve (strainer) with clean muslin (cheesecloth) and place over a large bowl. Ladle stock through sieve (strainer) and discard vegetables. Cover and store in the refrigerator for up to 3 days or freeze for up to 3 months.

Makes 1.55 litres (55 fl oz/7 cups)

BEAN CURD SOUP

1 litre (35 fl oz/4 cups) Singaporean Vegetable Stock
  (see page 12)
225 g (8 oz) bean curd, cut into 1 cm (½ in) cubes
1 fresh red chilli, cored, deseeded and finely chopped
6 shallots, finely chopped
1 small carrot, finely chopped
2 spring onions (scallions), sliced into rings
4 tablespoons light soy sauce
2 teaspoons light brown sugar
salt

Pour stock into a saucepan. Add bean curd, chilli, shallots, carrot, spring onions (scallions), soy sauce and sugar.

Bring to the boil, uncovered. Stir briefly then simmer for 2-3 minutes.

Add salt to taste. Ladle the soup into warmed soup bowls. Serve as part of a main meal to counterbalance hot dishes.

Serves 4.

VERMICELLI & MUSHROOM SOUP

1 tablespoon vegetable oil
½ teaspoon minced garlic
½ tablespoon finely chopped fresh root ginger
1 tablespoon chopped spring onion
1 litre (35 fl oz/4½ cups) Singaporean Vegetable
   Stock (see page 12) or water
2 tablespoons soy sauce
1 tablespoon sugar
55 g (2 oz) dried bean curd skins, soaked then cut
   into small pieces
55 g (2 oz) bean thread vermicelli, soaked then cut
   into short lengths
8-10 Chinese dried mushrooms, soaked and sliced
salt and freshly ground black pepper
fresh coriander sprigs, to garnish

Heat oil in a wok or pan and stir-fry garlic, ginger and spring onions for 20 seconds, or until fragrant. Add the stock or water and bring to a rolling boil. Add the soy sauce and sugar and simmer for about 30 seconds. (The soup can be made in advance up to this point, then brought back to the boil.)

Add the bean curd skins, vermicelli and mushrooms and cook for 2-3 minutes. Adjust the seasoning and serve garnished with coriander sprigs.

Serves 4-6.

Variation: For non-vegetarians, add 1-2 tablespoons dried shrimps, soaked, if wished. Chicken or meat stock can be used instead of vegetable stock.

MIXED VEGETABLE SOUP

1 tablespoon vegetable oil
1 teaspoon minced garlic
1 small onion, chopped
1 teaspoon chilli sauce
1 tablespoon sugar
685 ml (24 fl oz/3 cups) Singaporean Vegetable
   Stock (see page 12) or water
2 tablespoons soy sauce
3 tablespoons tamarind water or 2 tablespoons lime juice
1 cake bean curd, cut into small cubes
225 g (8 oz) bok choy (Chinese cabbage) or spinach,
   chopped
175 g (6 oz) bean sprouts
3-4 firm tomatoes, cut into thin wedges
salt and freshly ground black pepper
5-6 fresh basil leaves, coarsely chopped

Heat oil in a wok or pan and stir-fry garlic and onion for about 30 seconds. Add the chilli sauce and sugar and stir to make into a smooth paste. Add the stock or water, bring to boil, then add soy sauce and tamarind water or lime juice; simmer for 1 minute. (The soup can be made in advance up to this point.)

Bring the soup back to a rolling boil and add bean curd, bok choy, bean sprouts and tomatoes. Cook for about 2 minutes. Adjust seasoning and serve the soup piping hot, garnished with chopped basil leaves.

Serves 4-6.

SEAFOOD & COCONUT SOUP

CHICKEN & MUSHROOM SOUP

3 stalks lemon grass, cut into 5 cm (2 in) lengths
5 cm (2 in) piece galangal, thinly sliced
2.5 cm (1 in) piece fresh root ginger, thinly sliced
2 teaspoons finely chopped red chilli
1 litre (35 fl oz/4½ cups) coconut milk
10 kaffir lime leaves
200 g (7 oz) boneless, skinless chicken breast, cubed
5 tablespoons Thai fish sauce
juice of ½ lime
200 g (7 oz) raw unpeeled large prawns (jumbo shrimp), peeled and deveined
200 g (7 oz) firm white fish fillets, cubed
small handful each fresh coriander (cilantro) and Thai basil leaves
fresh coriander (cilantro) sprigs, to garnish

2 cloves garlic, crushed
4 coriander sprigs
1½ teaspoons black peppercorns, crushed
1 tablespoon vegetable oil
1 litre (35 fl oz/4¼ cups) Singaporean Chicken Stock (see page 11)
5 pieces dried Chinese black mushrooms, soaked in cold water for 20 minutes, drained and coarsely chopped
1 tablespoon fish sauce
115 g (4 oz) chicken, cut into strips
55 g (2 oz/¼ cup) spring onions (scallions), thinly sliced
fresh coriander (cilantro) sprigs, to garnish

In a saucepan, put lemon grass, galangal, ginger and chilli. Add 225 ml (8 fl oz/2 cups) water. Bring to a boil then simmer for 5 minutes. Add coconut milk and lime leaves. Simmer for 10 minutes. Add chicken, fish sauce and lime juice to pan. Poach for 5 minutes. Add prawns (shrimp) and fish. Poach for a further 2-3 minutes until prawns (shrimp) turn pink.

Using a pestle and mortar or small blender, pound or mix garlic, coriander stalks and leaves and peppercorns to a paste. In a wok, heat oil, add paste and cook, stirring, for 1 minute. Stir in stock, mushrooms and fish sauce. Simmer for 5 minutes.

Add coriander (cilantro) and basil to pan. Stir, then ladle into warm soup bowls. Remove and discard lemon grass and lime leaves before eating. Garnish with coriander (cilantro).

Serves 4.

Add chicken, lower heat so liquid barely moves and cook gently for 5 minutes. Scatter spring onions (scallions) over surface and garnish with coriander (cilantro) sprigs.

Serves 4.

CHICKEN DUMPLING SOUP

225 g (8 oz/1 cup) lean chicken, minced
1 tablespoon light soy sauce
3 tablespoons chopped fresh chives
1 clove garlic, finely chopped
2 egg whites
1 teaspoon caster sugar
salt and freshly ground black pepper
16 wonton skins
1 litre (35 fl oz/4½ cups) Singaporean Chicken
  Stock (see page 11)
2 tablespoons rice wine

HOT & SOUR TURKEY SOUP

115 g (4 oz/½ cup) lean turkey, minced
25 g (1 oz) dried Chinese mushrooms, soaked in hot
  water for 20 minutes
115 g (4 oz) Szechuan preserved vegetable, shredded
1 litre (35 fl oz/4½ cups) Singaporean Chicken
  Stock (see page 11)
2 teaspoons brown sugar
2 tablespoons red rice vinegar
large pinch ground white pepper
1 tablespoon dark soy sauce
2 teaspoons cornflour (cornstarch) blended with 4
  teaspoons water
2 spring onions (scallions), finely chopped
2 tablespoons chopped fresh coriander (cilantro)

In a bowl, mix the chicken, soy sauce, 1 tablespoon of the chives and the garlic. Bind together with 1 egg white and stir in sugar and seasoning.

Blanch the turkey in a saucepan of boiling water for 3 minutes. Drain and set aside. Drain mushrooms and squeeze out excess water. Discard stems and slice the caps.

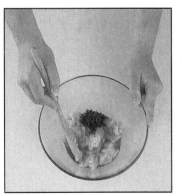

Place a little of the chicken mixture in the centre of each wonton skin, brush edges with egg white and bring the corners together, pinching the edges to seal. Cook dumplings in a large pan of boiling water for 1 minute. Drain. Bring stock to the boil and stir in the rice wine, dumplings and remaining chives. Simmer for 2 minutes. Serve immediately.

Serves 4.

Place all the ingredients except the cornflour (cornstarch) mixture, spring onions (scallions) and coriander (cilantro), in a saucepan. Bring to the boil and simmer for 3 minutes. Add the cornflour (cornstarch) mixture and cook, stirring, until thickened. Add chopped spring onions (scallions) and coriander (cilantro) and serve.

Serves 4.

CHICKEN & ASPARAGUS SOUP

225 g (8 oz) fresh asparagus
1 litre (35 fl oz/4½ cups) Singaporean Chicken
   Stock (see page 11)
2 tablespoons light soy sauce
2 tablespoons dry sherry
2 teaspoons brown sugar
55 g (2 oz) vermicelli rice noodles
1 cm (½ in) piece fresh root ginger, chopped
350 g (12 oz) lean cooked chicken, finely shredded
salt and ground white pepper
2 spring onions (scallions), finely chopped, to
   garnish

PAPAYA & PORK SOUP

1 litre (35 fl oz/4½ cups) stock or water
4 pork chops, each weighing about 85 g (3 oz)
1 small unripe green papaya, peeled and cut into
   small cubes
2 tablespoons Thai fish sauce
salt and freshly ground black pepper
1 tablespoon chopped spring onions (scallions)
fresh coriander (cilantro) sprigs, to garnish

Bring stock or water to the boil in a wok or pan and add the pork. Bring back to boil and skim off the scum, then reduce heat, cover and simmer gently for 25-30 minutes.

Trim ends from asparagus stalks and slice stalks into 4 cm (1½ in) pieces. Pour stock into a large saucepan along with soy sauce and sherry. Stir in brown sugar. Bring to the boil and add asparagus and noodles. Simmer, covered, for 5-6 minutes.

Add the papaya cubes and fish sauce, bring back to boil and cook the soup for a further 5 minutes.

Stir in the chopped ginger and shredded chicken and season well. Simmer gently for 3-4 minutes to heat through. Garnish with chopped spring onions (scallions) and serve.

Serves 4.

To serve, place salt, pepper and the chopped spring onions (scallions) in a tureen. Pour the boiling soup with its contents over it, garnish with coriander (cilantro) sprigs and serve at once. The meat should be so tender that one can easily tear it apart into small pieces for eating.

Serves 4.

CHICKEN NOODLE SOUP

2 tablespoons vegetable oil
4 shallots, sliced
1 clove garlic, chopped
225 g (8 oz) chicken thigh meat, shredded
115 g (4 oz) raw peeled prawns (shrimp)
3 sticks celery, sliced
½ teaspoon sugar
2 tablespoons chopped spring onions (scallions)
2 tablespoons Thai fish sauce
salt and freshly ground black pepper
1 litre (35 fl oz/4½ cups) chicken stock
250 g (9 oz) dried rice sticks, cooked in boiling
    water for 4-5 minutes, drained
2 tablespoons crushed peanuts
fresh coriander (cilantro) sprigs, to garnish

Heat oil in a wok or frying pan (skillet) and stir-fry shallots and garlic for about 30 seconds until fragrant. Add chicken and prawns (shrimp), stir-fry for 1 more minute, then add the celery and continue stirring for a further 2 minutes. Add sugar, about half of the spring onions (scallions) and fish sauce, and season with salt and pepper. Blend well and set aside.

Bring chicken stock to a rolling boil with the remaining spring onions (scallions) and fish sauce. Place a portion of rice sticks in each of 4 individual serving bowls, put some chicken, prawns (shrimp) and celery on top, then pour the stock over the top. Garnish with peanuts and coriander (cilantro) and serve hot, with additional seasonings if wished.

Serves 4.

BEEF & WATER CHESTNUT SOUP

350 g (12 oz) lean rump or sirloin steak
1 litre (35 fl oz/4½ cups) Singaporean Beef Stock,
    (see page 11)
1 cinnamon stick, broken
2 star anise
2 tablespoons dark soy sauce
2 tablespoons dry sherry
3 tablespoons tomato purée (paste)
1-2 teaspoons chilli sauce
115 g (4 oz) canned water chestnuts, rinsed and
    sliced
2 spring onions (scallions), chopped, to garnish

Trim away any fat from beef and cut into thin strips.

Place all the ingredients except the spring onions (scallions) in a large saucepan. Bring to the boil, skimming away surface scum with a flat ladle. Cover and simmer gently for 20 minutes until beef is tender.

Skim soup again and discard cinnamon stick and star anise. Blot surface with kitchen paper to remove fat. Garnish with spring onions (scallions) and serve.

Serves 4.

BEEF & RICE NOODLE SOUP

1.35 kg (3 lb) oxtail, cut into pieces
2 stalks lemon grass, chopped
1 large piece fresh root ginger
1 onion, sliced
5-6 whole star anise
6 cloves
1 cinnamon stick (optional)
1 tablespoon sugar
1 teaspoon salt
2 tablespoons Thai fish sauce
450 g (1 lb) flat rice noodles, soaked in hot water
  for 10 minutes, then drained
225-300 g (8-10 oz) sirloin beef steak, cut into
  small paper-thin slices

SOUP ACCOMPANIMENTS:
115 g (4 oz/1 cup) bean sprouts
½ cucumber, thinly shredded
4-5 lettuce leaves, shredded
1 onion, thinly sliced
4 small red chillies, deseeded and chopped
2 limes, cut into wedges
fresh mint, basil and coriander (cilantro) leaves
chilli sauce

Arrange the accompaniments on a serving platter. Place a portion of the rice noodles in each of 4-6 large individual serving bowls.

Trim off as much excess fat from oxtail as possible. Place pieces in a large pot, add lemon grass, ginger, onion, star anise, cloves, and cinnamon stick, if using. Add 2 litre (70 fl oz/9 cups) water and bring to the boil. Reduce heat and simmer oxtail for at least 2½ hours, skimming the surface occasionally to remove the scum.

Bring the beef broth to a rolling boil. Place a few slices of beef steak on top of noodles and pour in the boiling broth to fill the bowls about three-quarters full. Take them to the table.

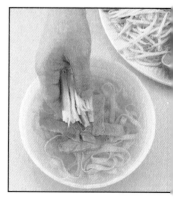

Strain the stock and discard the oxtail and flavouring ingredients (the meat from the bones can be used for another dish). Add sugar, salt, and fish sauce to the clear stock, bring back to the boil and simmer for 2-3 minutes. (At this stage, the stock can be cooled and refrigerated for 1-2 days. The fat can be removed from the top and the stock reheated ready for use.)

Each person takes a small amount of bean sprouts, cucumber, lettuce, onion, chillies, and herbs and places them on top of the noodles, with a squeeze of lime and more seasonings as desired.

Serves 4-6

Note: This is almost a meal on its own, and is traditionally eaten as breakfast, lunch or as a snack at any time of the day.

PRAWN CRYSTAL ROLLS

225 g (8 oz) cooked peeled prawns (shrimp)
115 g (4 oz) cooked pork, coarsely chopped
115 g (4 oz) cooked chicken meat, coarsely chopped
2 tablespoons grated carrot
2 tablespoons chopped water chestnuts
1 tablespoon chopped preserved vegetable
1 teaspoon finely chopped garlic
2 spring onions (scallions), finely chopped
1 teaspoon sugar
2 tablespoons Thai fish sauce
salt and freshly ground black pepper
10-12 sheets dried rice paper
flour and water paste
fresh mint and coriander leaves
Iceberg or Webb's lettuce leaves
Spicy Fish Sauce (see page 121)

Cut any large prawns (shrimp) in half. In a bowl, mix prawns (shrimp), pork, chicken, grated carrot, water chestnuts, preserved vegetable, garlic, spring onions (scallions), sugar, fish sauce and salt and pepper. Fill a bowl with warm water, then dip the sheets of rice paper in the water one at a time. If using large sheets of rice paper, fold in half then place about 2 tablespoons of the filling on to the long end of the rice paper, fold the sides over to enclose the filling and roll up, then seal the end with a little of the flour paste. The roll will be transparent, hence the name 'crystal'.

To serve, place some mint and coriander in a piece of lettuce leaf with a crystal roll and wrap into a neat package, then dip the roll into the spicy fish sauce before eating.

Serves 4.

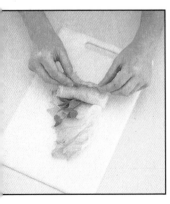

GINGERED MELONS

½ honeydew melon
½ cantaloupe melon
115 g (4 oz) canned water chestnuts, rinsed
2.5 cm (1 in) piece fresh root ginger, finely chopped
4 tablespoons dry sherry
4 pieces stem ginger in syrup, sliced
2 tablespoons dried melon seeds

Using a spoon, scoop out the seeds from both melons. Cut in half, peel away skin and thinly slice melon flesh. Slice water chestnuts.

Arrange melon slices on serving plates and top with sliced water chestnuts.

Mix together chopped ginger, dry sherry and stem ginger with its syrup and spoon over melon and water chestnuts. Cover and chill for 30 minutes. Sprinkle with melon seeds and serve.

Serves 4.

CHILLI CUCUMBER SALAD

450 g (1 lb) cucumber
2 teaspoons salt
1 green pepper (capsicum)
2 tablespoons sesame seeds
strips of fresh red chilli, to garnish
Dressing:
2 shallots, finely chopped
1 fresh red chilli, deseeded and chopped
3 tablespoons white rice vinegar
1 tablespoon rice wine
2 teaspoons caster sugar
2 teaspoons light soy sauce
1 teaspoon sesame oil

MARINATED MUSHROOMS

25 g (1 oz) dried Chinese mushrooms, soaked in hot
  water for 20 minutes
115 g (4 oz) oyster mushrooms
115 g (4 oz) button mushrooms
1 tablespoon sunflower oil
2 tablespoons light soy sauce
2 sticks celery, chopped
2 cloves garlic, thinly sliced
1 cinnamon stick, broken
chopped celery leaves, to garnish
Marinade:
3 tablespoons light soy sauce
3 tablespoons dry sherry
freshly ground black pepper

Peel cucumber and slice very thinly. Place in a bowl, sprinkle with the salt and set aside for 15 minutes. Halve and seed the pepper (capsicum) and thinly slice lengthwise.

Drain Chinese mushrooms and squeeze out excess water. Discard stems and thinly slice caps. Slice oyster and button mushrooms. Heat oil in a non-stick or well seasoned wok and stir-fry all the mushrooms for 2 minutes.

Mix together the dressing ingredients. Rinse the cucumber slices, drain well and pat dry with kitchen paper. Place in a bowl and carefully mix in the green pepper (capsicum). Pour over the dressing, cover and chill for 1 hour. Mix well, sprinkle with sesame seeds, garnish with chilli strips and serve.

Serves 4.

Add remaining ingredients except marinade and garnish and stir-fry for 2-3 minutes until just cooked. Transfer to a shallow dish and leave to cool. Mix together marinade ingredients and pour over cooled mushroom mixture. cover and chill for 1 hour. Discard cinnamon stick, garnish and serve on a bed of bean sprouts and shredded Chinese leaves.

Serves 4.

CURRY PUFFS

225 g (8 oz/1 cup) unsalted butter
600 g (1 lb 4 oz/4 cups) plain (all-purpose) flour
salt
3 tablespoons vegetable oil plus extra for deep-frying
4 shallots, thinly sliced
2 cloves garlic, finely crushed
1 teaspoon grated fresh root ginger
1 fresh green chilli, cored, deseeded and finely chopped
4 teaspoons curry powder
450 g (1 lb/2 cups) minced (ground) beef, lamb or chicken
1 potato, finely diced
1 tablespoon lime juice, or to taste
6 tablespoons chopped celery leaves
celery leaves, to garnish

Melt butter with 2 tablespoons water. In a bowl, combine butter mixture with flour, pinch of salt and about 6 tablespoons water to give a medium-soft dough. Transfer to a work surface and knead for about 10 minutes. Form into a ball. Brush with oil and put in a plastic bag. Leave for at least 30 minutes.

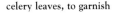

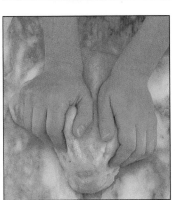

Heat oil in a frying pan (skillet). Add shallots and fry for 4-5 minutes until browned. Stir in garlic, ginger, chilli and curry powder for 30 seconds. Add meat. Cook until pale, stirring to break up lumps. Stir in potato, lime juice, salt to taste and 2 tablespoons water. Simmer gently, covered, for 15-20 minutes until meat and potatoes are tender.

Add celery leaves and cook for 2 minutes. If necessary, increase heat and boil to drive off excess moisture, stirring. Knead dough. Break off a 2.5 cm (1 in) piece. Form into a smooth ball then roll to a 10 cm (4 in) disc.

Put 2 teaspoons meat mixture along centre. Brush half of edges of dough circle with water and fold dough over filling.

Pinch edges together to seal. Place, pinched end up, on a plate. Repeat with remaining filling and dough. Heat enough oil for deep-frying in a wok or deep-fryer over medium-low heat. Add a few curry puffs so they are not crowded and fry slowly until golden; turn them over so they cook evenly. Remove with a slotted spoon and drain on paper towels. Serve warm, garnished with celery leaves.

Makes about 30.

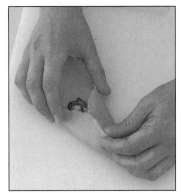

NONYA PACKETS

4 dried Chinese black mushrooms
225 g (8 oz) boneless, skinless chicken breast, thinly
  sliced into strips
1 tablespoon oyster sauce
1½ teaspoons rice wine
1½ teaspoons sesame oil
1 cm (½ in) piece fresh root ginger, grated
1½ teaspoons light soy sauce
1 clove garlic, finely crushed
½ fresh red chilli, cored, deseeded and finely chopped
2 spring onions (scallions), including some green,
  chopped

Soak mushrooms in 3 tablespoons hot water
for 30 minutes. Drain. Discard stems and
finely slice caps.

Soak mushrooms in 3 tablespoons hot water
for 30 minutes. Drain. Discard stems and
finely slice caps.

In a bowl, mix chicken, oyster sauce, rice
wine, sesame oil, ginger, soy sauce, garlic and
chilli. Cover and leave in a cool place for up
to 1 hour, or in the refrigerator up to 8 hours
(return to room temperature 30 minutes
before cooking). Cut 10 15 × 15 cm (6 in)
squares of greaseproof paper. Lay 1 on the
work surface with a point towards you. Put
several pieces of chicken near the point.
Add some mushroom strips and spring
onions (scallions). Fold the point over the
filling, making a firm crease. Fold the left and
right hand corners to the middle.

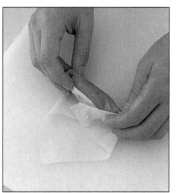

Continue to fold the package over, away
from you. Tuck in the last flap to make a
package about 7.5 × 5 cm (3 × 2 in). Repeat
with remaining chicken and greaseproof
paper. Half fill a wok or deep fryer with oil
and heat to 185-190C (360-375F). Fry packets in batches for about 8 minutes, pushing
them under occasionally and turning over
once or twice. Remove with a slotted spoon.
Keep warm while cooking remaining pack-
ages. Serve unopened.

Serves 5-6.

GRILLED CHICKEN SKEWERS

6 large chicken thighs, total weight about 1 kg (2¼ lb)
2 cloves garlic, finely chopped
150 ml (5 fl oz/⅔ cup) coconut milk
2 teaspoons ground coriander
1 teaspoon each ground cumin and ground turmeric
juice of 1 lime
leaves from 8 sprigs coriander, chopped
3 tablespoons light soy sauce
2 tablespoons Thai fish sauce
3 tablespoons light brown sugar
½ teaspoon crushed dried chillies

mix in (handwritten note)
sauce (handwritten note)

Using a sharp knife, slit along underside of
each chicken thigh and remove bone, scrap-
ing flesh from bone.

Cut each boned thigh into 6 pieces. Put in a
bowl. In a small bowl, mix together garlic,
coconut milk, coriander, cumin and
turmeric. Pour over chicken. Stir to coat
then cover and refrigerate for 2-12 hours. To
make a sauce, in a small serving bowl, mix
together remaining ingredients. Set aside.

Soak 8 short wooden or bamboo skewers for
30 minutes. Preheat grill (broiler). Thread
chicken, skin side up, on skewers. Put on
oiled grilled (broiler) rack and cool for 4-5
minutes. Turn over and cook for further 2-3
minutes until juices run clear. Serve with
sauce.

Serves 4-6.

SEAFOOD SKEWERS

12 scallops
12 large raw peeled prawns (shrimp)
225 g (8 oz) firm white fish fillet, such as halibut,
  cod or monkfish, cut into 12 cubes
1 onion, cut into 12 pieces
1 red or green pepper (capsicum), cut into 12 cubes
115 ml (4 fl oz/½ cup) dry white wine or sherry
1 tablespoon chopped fresh dill
1 tablespoon chopped fresh holy basil leaves
1 tablespoon lime juice or vinegar
salt and freshly ground black pepper
vegetable oil, for brushing
Spicy Fish Sauce, page 121, to serve

In a bowl, mix scallops, prawns (shrimp), fish, onion and pepper (capsicum) with the wine, dill, basil, lime juice or vinegar, salt and pepper. Leave to marinate in a cool place for 2-3 hours, the longer the better. Meanwhile, soak 6 bamboo skewers in hot water for 25-30 minutes and prepare a barbecue or preheat grill. Thread seafood and vegetables alternately on to the skewers so that each skewer has 2 pieces of every ingredient.

Brush each filled skewer with a little oil and cook on barbecue or under the hot grill (broiler) for 5-6 minutes, turning frequently. Serve hot with the fish sauce as a dip.

Serves 6.

STUFFED COURGETTES

55 g (2 oz/½ cup) fresh coconut, grated
6 tablespoons chopped fresh coriander (cilantro)
  leaves
1 fresh green chilli, deseeded and finely chopped
4 courgettes (zucchini), each about 225 g (8 oz)
5 tablespoons vegetable oil
few drops Thai fish sauce
2 tablespoons lime juice
1 teaspoon crushed palm sugar
freshly ground black pepper

In a small bowl, combine coconut, coriander and chilli; set aside.

Cut each courgette (zucchini) into 4 lengths, about 4 cm (1½ in) long. Stand each on one cut side and cut 2 deep slits like a cross, down 2.5 cm (1 in) of the length. Gently prise apart cut sections and fill with coconut mixture. Pour oil and 115 ml (4 fl oz/½ cup) water into a wide frying pan (skillet). Stand courgettes (zucchini), filled side uppermost, in pan.

Sprinkle over a little fish sauce. If any coconut mixture remains, spoon over courgettes (zucchini). Sprinkle over lime juice, sugar, black pepper and a few drops of fish sauce. Heat to simmering point, cover tightly and simmer gently for 5-6 minutes. Using 2 spoons, turn courgette (zucchini) pieces over, re-cover and cook for a further 7-10 minutes so some 'bite' is retained.

Serves 4-6.

PRAWN BALLS

700 g (1½ lb) raw, unpeeled large prawns (jumbo shrimp)
1 clove garlic, chopped
1½ tablespoons fish sauce
½ teaspoon light brown sugar
2 teaspoons groundnut oil
1 tablespoon cornflour (cornstarch)
1 egg, beaten
salt and freshly ground black pepper
45 g (1½ oz) desiccated (unsweetened shredded) coconut
2 tablespoons dried breadcrumbs
fresh coriander (cilantro) sprigs, to garnish
Dipping Sauce or Spicy Sauce (see page 120)

Reserve 8 prawns (shrimp) in their shells. Peel remaining prawns (shrimp).

With the point of a sharp knife, cut a slit along the back of each peeled prawn (shrimp). Remove and discard black intestinal thread. Put prawns (shrimp) in a food processor. Add garlic, fish sauce, sugar, oil, cornflour (cornstarch), egg, salt and pepper. Mix to a smooth purée. Transfer to a bowl, cover and chill for 1½ hours.

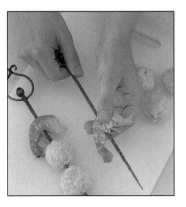

Preheat grill (broiler). On a baking sheet, combine coconut and breadcrumbs. Wet the palms of your hands; roll the prawn (shrimp) mixture into 2.5 cm (1 in) balls. Coat balls in coconut mixture. Thread on oiled, long metal skewers, adding a reserved prawn (shrimp) to each skewer. Grill (broil), turning occasionally, for about 6 minutes until balls are firm and whole prawns (shrimp) are pink. Garnish and serve with dipping sauce of your choice.

Serves 8.

CRISPY WONTONS

1 red pepper (capsicum)
1 carrot
115 g (4 oz) each button mushrooms and bean sprouts
5 spring onions (scallions)
550 ml (20 fl oz/2½ cups) sunflower oil
1 teaspoon grated fresh root ginger
1 teaspoon sugar
1 teaspoon each soy sauce and sesame oil
2 teaspoons sherry
24 wonton skins
Dipping sauce:
6 tablespoons lime juice
2 teaspoons sugar
1 teaspoon Thai fish sauce
1 teaspoon finely chopped spring onion (scallions)
1 fresh green chilli, cored, deseeded and chopped

To make dipping sauce, mix together lime juice, sugar, fish sauce, spring onion (scallion) and chilli. Stir until sugar has dissolved. Set aside. Cut pepper (capsicum) and carrot into thin matchsticks. Thinly slice mushrooms. Shred spring onions (scallions), reserving a few shreds for garnish. Heat 2 tablespoons sunflower oil in a wok and stir-fry pepper (capsicum), carrot, mushrooms, bean sprouts, spring onions (scallions) and ginger for 1 minute. Add sugar, soy sauce, sesame oil and sherry and cook, stirring, for 2 minutes. Turn into a sieve (strainer) and leave to drain and cool.

Put 1 teaspoon vegetable mixture in the middle of each wonton skin. Gather up corners and twist together to seal. In a wok or deep-fat fryer, heat oil to 180C (350F) or until a cube of bread browns in 60 seconds. Fry wontons, a few at a time, for 1-2 minutes, until crisp and golden. Remove with a slotted spoon and drain on kitchen paper. Keep warm while frying remaining wontons. Garnish with reserved spring onion shreds (scallions) and serve with dipping sauce.

Serves 6.

SESAME PRAWN SALAD

STUFFED EGGS

225 g (8 oz) mange tout (snow peas)
55 g (2 oz) oyster mushrooms, thinly sliced
115 g (4 oz) canned water chestnuts, rinsed and
   sliced
225 g (8 oz) cooked, peeled prawns (shrimp),
   thawed and dried, if frozen
2 tablespoons sesame seeds
Dressing:
1 tablespoon sesame oil
1 tablespoon light soy sauce
2 teaspoons white rice vinegar
1 teaspoon brown sugar
salt and freshly ground black pepper

4 large eggs, at room temperature
4 tablespoons minced ground cooked pork
4 tablespoons finely chopped peeled prawns (shrimp)
1 teaspoon Thai fish sauce
1 clove garlic, finely chopped
1½ tablespoons chopped coriander leaves
freshly ground black pepper
lettuce leaves, to serve
fresh coriander (cilantro) sprigs, to garnish

Form 4 'nests' from foil to hold eggs upright. Place in a steaming basket. Cook eggs in pan of gently boiling water for 1½ minutes; remove.

Top and tail the mange tout (snow peas) and string if necessary. Bring a saucepan of water to the boil and cook for 2 minutes until just softened. Drain and rinse under cold water. Drain and leave to cool completely.

Carefully peel a small part of pointed end of eggs. With the point of a slim, sharp knife, cut a small hole down through the exposed white of each egg; reserve pieces of white that are removed. Pour liquid egg yolk and white from egg into a small bowl. Thoroughly mix in pork, prawns (shrimp), fish sauce, garlic, coriander and pepper. Carefully spoon into eggs and replace removed pieces of white.

Mix together the sliced mushrooms, water chestnuts, prawns (shrimp) and sesame seeds. Stir in the cooled mange tout (snow peas). Mix together the dressing ingredients and pour over the salad just before serving.

Serves 4.

Set steaming basket over a saucepan of boiling water and place eggs, cut end uppermost, in foil 'nests'. Cover basket and steam eggs for about 12 minutes. When cool enough to handle, carefully peel off shells. Serve whole or halved on lettuce leaves, garnished with coriander (cilantro) sprigs.

Serves 4.

STEAMED CRAB

1 clove garlic, chopped
1 small shallot, chopped
6 fresh coriander (cilantro) sprigs, stalks finely
    chopped
175 g (6 oz) cooked crabmeat *OR shrimp*
115 g (4 oz) lean pork, very finely chopped and
    cooked
1 egg, beaten
1 tablespoon coconut cream
2 teaspoons Thai fish sauce
freshly ground black pepper
1 fresh red chilli, deseeded and cut into fine strips

Grease 4 individual heatproof dishes and
place in a steaming basket.

Using a pestle and mortar, pound garlic,
shallot and coriander stalks to a paste. In a
bowl, stir together crabmeat, pork, garlic
paste, egg, coconut cream, fish sauce and
plenty of black pepper until evenly mixed.

Divide between dishes, arrange coriander
(cilantro) leaves and strips of chilli on tops.
Place steaming basket over a saucepan of
boiling water and steam for about 12 minutes
until mixture is firm.

Serves 4.

Note: Crab shells may be used instead of
dishes for cooking.

STEAMED OPEN DIM SUM

115 g (4 oz) bean curd, drained and mashed
2 spring onions (scallions), finely chopped
1 stick celery, finely chopped
1 tablespoon chopped fresh coriander (cilantro)
1 cm (½ in) piece fresh root ginger, finely chopped
2 teaspoons light soy sauce
salt and freshly ground black pepper
16 wonton skins
fresh coriander leaves (cilantro) to garnish

Put all the ingredients except the wonton
skins and garnish into a bowl and mix
together until well combined. Spoon a portion on to each wonton skin.

Dampen wonton skins with water. Bring up
the sides of each wonton, pressing them
around the filling and leaving the tops open.
Flatten the bottoms.

Bring a wok or large saucepan of water to the
boil. Place wontons on a sheet of baking
parchment in a steamer and place over the
water. Cover and steam for 15 minutes.
Garnish with coriander (cilantro) and serve
on a bed of rice, with chilli sauce as a dip.

Serves 4.

CRAB ROLLS

225 g (8 oz) cooked chicken, very finely chopped
115 g (4 oz/½ cup) cooked crabmeat, flaked
4 spring onions (scallions), finely chopped
25 g (1 oz/½) beansprouts, finely chopped
1 small carrot, grated
2 teaspoons Thai fish sauce
freshly ground black pepper
about 9 rice paper wrappers, each about 18 cm
  (7 in) in diameter
vegetable oil, for deep frying
fresh Thai holy basil leaves, Thai mint leaves and
  lettuce leaves, to serve
Dipping Sauce (see page 120)

In a bowl, mix together chicken, crabmeat, spring onions (scallions), beansprouts, carrot, fish sauce and black pepper. Brush both sides of each wrapper liberally with water and set aside to soften. Cut each into 4 wedges. Place a small amount of filling near wide end of one wedge, fold end over filling, tuck in sides and roll up. Repeat with remaining wedges and filling.

In a wok, heat oil to 190C (375F). Fry rolls in batches for 2-3 minutes until crisp and golden. Drain on absorbent kitchen paper. Serve hot. To eat, sprinkle each roll with herbs, then wrap in a lettuce leaf and dip into dipping sauce.

Makes about 36.

PRAWN OMELETTE

6 eggs
1 teaspoon Thai fish sauce
2 teaspoons light brown sugar
1 tablespoon groundnut oil
85 g (3 oz) bamboo shoots, finely chopped
1 clove garlic, finely chopped
1 teaspoon grated fresh root ginger
2 spring onions (scallions), including a little green,
  thinly sliced
2 tablespoons chopped fresh coriander (cilantro)
175 g (6 oz) shelled cooked prawns (shrimp)
fresh coriander (cilantro) sprigs, to garnish

In a medium bowl, beat eggs with fish sauce and sugar. Set aside.

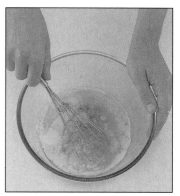

In a wok or frying pan (skillet) heat ½ of oil. Add bamboo shoots, garlic, ginger and spring onions (scallions). Fry for about 2 minutes. Remove pan from heat and stir in coriander (cilantro) and prawns (shrimp). Add to egg mixture and stir together. In a frying pan (skillet), heat remaining oil. Stir egg mixture then pour evenly over base of pan. Lower heat and leave to cook until underside is set and golden brown and top is almost set.

Put a warm plate upside down on pan. Invert the pan and plate together so the omelette falls on to plate. Using a fish slice, slide omelette back into pan and cook until underside is brown. Cut into wedges and garnish with coriander (cilantro) sprigs.

Serves 3-4.

SEAFOOD DISHES

FISH WITH LEMON GRASS

2 tablespoons vegetable oil
1 flat fish, such as pomfret, plump lemon sole,
  flouder or plaice, gutted and cleaned
4 cloves garlic, finely chopped
2 fresh red chillies, deseeded and finely chopped
1 red shallot, chopped
4½ tablespoons lime juice
½ teaspoon crushed palm sugar
½ tablespoons finely chopped lemon grass
2 teaspoons Thai fish sauce
chilli flowers, to garnish

In a wok, heat oil, add fish, skin-side down first, and cook for 3-5 minutes a side until lightly browned and lightly cooked. Using a fish slice, transfer to a warmed serving plate, cover and keep warm. Add garlic to wok and fry, stirring occasionally, until browned.

Stir in chillies, shallot, lime juice, sugar, lemon grass and fish sauce. Allow to simmer gently for 1-2 minutes. Pour over fish and garnish with chilli flowers.

Serves 2.

STEAMED FISH CAKES

1 cm (½ in) piece fresh root ginger, peeled and
  chopped
700 g (1½ lb) cod fillets, skinned and chopped
1 egg white, lightly beaten
2 teaspoons cornflour (cornstarch)
2 tablespoons chopped fresh chives
salt and ground white pepper
115 g (4 oz) oyster mushrooms
2 shallots
225 g (8 oz) courgettes (zucchini)
1 red pepper (capsicum), halved
1 yellow pepper (capsicum), halved
1 cm (½ in) piece fresh root ginger
1 clove garlic
fresh chives, to garnish

Put the chopped ginger, cod, egg white, cornflour (cornstarch), chopped chives and seasoning in a food processor or blender and work until they form a firm mixture. Divide mixture into 12 portions and shape into 7.5 cm (3 in) diameter patties. Line a large plate with baking parchment, arrange fish cakes on plate, cover and chill for 30 minutes. Using a sharp knife, thinly slice the mushrooms, shallots, courgettes (zucchini), peppers (capsicum), remaining ginger and garlic.

Bring a wok or large saucepan of water to the boil. Arrange the vegetables on baking parchment in a steamer, place fish cakes on top and place over the water. Cover and steam for 10 minutes until cooked, turning fish cakes halfway through. Garnish with chives and serve with salad and oyster sauce.

Serves 4.

FISH WITH MUSHROOM SAUCE

plain (all-purpose) flour
salt and freshly ground black pepper
1 whole flat fish, such as pomfret, plump lemon
  soles, flounder or plaice, about 700 g (1½ lb),
  gutted and cleaned
2 tablespoons vegetable oil plus extra for deep frying
3 cloves garlic, thinly sliced
1 small onion, halved and thinly sliced
4 cm (1¾ in) piece fresh root ginger, finely chopped
115 g (4 oz) shiitake mushrooms, sliced
2 teaspoons Thai fish sauce
3 spring onions (scallions), sliced

Season flour with salt and pepper, then use to lightly dust fish. Heat oil in a large deep fat frying pan to 180C (350F), add fish and cook for 4-5 minutes, turning halfway through, until crisp and browned.

Meanwhile, heat 2 tablespoons oil in a wok, add garlic, onion and ginger and cook, stirring occasionally, for 2 minutes. Add mushrooms and stir-fry for 2 minutes. Stir in fish sauce, 3-4 tablespoons water and spring onions (scallions). Bubble briefly. Using a fish slice, transfer fish to absorbent kitchen paper to drain. Put on a warmed serving plate and spoon over sauce. Garnish with spring onion (scallion) brushes.

Serves 2.

FISH STEAKS WITH CHILLI

5 dried red chillies, cored and deseeded
½ small red pepper (capsicum), chopped
5 shallots, chopped
4 cloves garlic, chopped
4 tablespoons vegetable oil
450 g (1 lb) fish steaks such as cod, monkfish,
  salmon or snapper
fresh coriander (cilantro) sprigs, to garnish
rice and lime juice, to serve

Put chillies in a blender. Pour 4 tablespoons hot water over and leave until softened. Add red pepper (capsicum), shallots and garlic. Mix to a coarse paste.

In a frying pan (skillet) over medium heat, heat 2 tablespoons oil. Add fish and fry until lightly browned on both sides and almost, but not quite, cooked through. Using a fish slice, transfer to paper towels to drain.

Add remaining oil to pan. Add chilli paste and cook over medium-high heat for about 3 minutes until paste looks dryish. Stir in 2 tablespoons water. Lower heat, return fish to pan and baste with chilli paste. Cook gently for 1-2 minutes, basting with paste. Garnish with coriander (cilantro), and serve with rice and with plenty of lime juice squeezed over.

Serves 3-4.

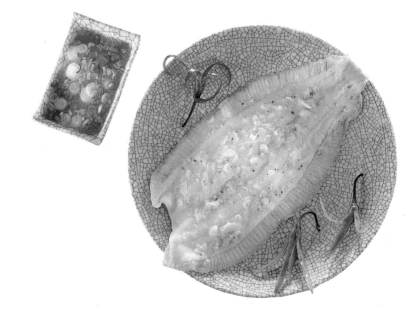

MILD FISH CURRY

3 small onions, chopped
2 cloves garlic, smashed
1 fresh red chilli, cored, deseeded and chopped
2.5 cm (1 in) piece of fresh root ginger, chopped
2 stalks lemon grass, chopped
2 teaspoons ground turmeric
3 tablespoons groundnut oil
500 ml (18 fl oz/2¼ cups) coconut milk
450 g (1 lb) firm white fish fillet, such as cod,
  haddock or monkfish, skinned and cubed
3 tablespoons thick coconut milk
55 g (2 oz/½ cup) desiccated (unsweetened
  shredded) coconut, dry-fried and pounded,
  see page 8-9
shredded fresh red chilli, to garnish

Put onions, garlic, chilli, ginger, lemon grass and turmeric in a blender and mix to a paste. Heat oil in a wok or frying pan (skillet) over medium-high heat. Add spice paste and fry for 3-4 minutes until fragrant but not coloured.

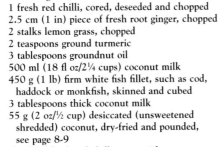

Stir coconut milk into spice paste. Bring to a boil, stirring, then lower heat and simmer for 3 minutes. Add fish to pan and cook gently for 3-4 minutes until just cooked through. Stir in thick coconut milk and pounded coconut. Serve garnished with shredded chilli.

Serves 3-4.

CORIANDER FISH & GARLIC

6 coriander roots, chopped
3 large cloves garlic, chopped
5 black peppercorns, crushed
2 fish fillets, such as trout or plaice
2 pieces banana leaf (optional)
3 tablespoons lime juice
½ teaspoon crushed palm sugar
1 spring onion (scallion), finely chopped
½ small fresh green chilli, deseeded and thinly sliced
½ small fresh red chilli, deseeded and thinly sliced
chilli flowers, to garnish

Using a pestle and mortar or small blender, briefly mix together coriander roots, garlic and peppercorns. Spread evenly over inside of fish fillets; set aside for 30 minutes.

Wrap fish in banana leaves or pieces of foil, securing leaf with wooden cocktail stick (toothpick), or folding edges of foil tightly together. Grill (broil) for about 8 minutes. Meanwhile, in a bowl, stir together lime juice and sugar, then stir in spring onion (scallion) and chillies. Serve with fish. Garnish with chilli flowers.

Serves 2.

FISH WITH GINGER

FRIED FISH FILLET

6 tablespoons vegetable oil
1 kg (2½ lb) whole white fish or single piece, such
  as cod, bass or red snapper
1 small onion, finely chopped
6 spring onions (scallions), thickly sliced
2 cloves garlic, crushed
1 tablespoon grated fresh root ginger
2 teaspoons Thai fish sauce
1½ tablespoons light soy sauce
1 teaspoon crushed palm sugar
1 tablespoon tamarind water, see page 8-9   *lime juice*
freshly ground black pepper
fresh coriander (cilantro) sprigs, to garnish

450 g (1 lb) firm white fish fillet, such as halibut, cod,
  haddock or monkfish, cut into 2 cm (¾ in) pieces
salt and freshly ground black pepper
1 egg, beaten
3 tablespoons plain (all-purpose) flour mixed with
  2 tablespoons water
vegetable oil for deep-frying
fresh holy basil and coriander (cilantro) sprigs, to
  garnish
Spicy Fish Sauce, page 121, to serve

In a dish, season the fish with salt and pepper and leave for 25-30 minutes. Make a batter by blending the beaten egg with the flour and water paste.

Over a medium heat, heat 4 tablespoons oil in a wok. Add fish and fry for about 5 minutes a side until browned and flesh flakes easily when flaked with a knife. Meanwhile, heat remaining oil in a small saucepan over a moderate heat, add onion and cook, stirring occasionally, until browned. When fish is cooked, transfer to absorbent kitchen paper and keep warm.

Heat oil in a wok or deep-fat fryer to 180C (350F). Coat the fish pieces with batter and deep-fry them, in batches, for 3-4 minutes until golden. Remove and drain.

Stir into wok, spring onions (scallions), garlic and ginger. Stir-fry for 2-3 minutes, then stir in fish sauce, soy sauce, palm sugar and tamarind water. Cook for 1 minute, season with black pepper, then pour over fish. Sprinkle over the browned onions and garnish with coriander.

Serves 4.

Place the fish pieces on a warmed serving dish with the garnishes. Serve at once with the spicy fish sauce as a dip.

Serves 4.

Variation: A whole fish, boned, skinned and coated in batter, can be deep-fried first then cut into bite-sized pieces for serving.

SMOKY GARLIC FISH STEW

700 g (1½ lb) firm white fish fillets, e.g. cod, huss or
  monkfish, skinned and cut into 2.5 cm (1 in)
  cubes
2 teaspoons light soy sauce
3 tablespoons ginger wine
1 tablespoon cornflour (cornstarch)
4 large cloves garlic
1 tablespoon sunflower oil
225 g (8 oz) shallots, sliced
2 tablespoons fermented black beans
4 spring onions (scallions), cut into 2.5 cm (1 in)
  pieces
2 tablespoons dark soy sauce

In a bowl, mix together the cubed fish, light
soy sauce, ginger wine and cornflour (cornstarch). Roughly chop the garlic and add to
the fish mixture. Cover and chill for 30
minutes. Heat oil in a non-stick or well seasoned wok and stir-fry fish mixture and shallots for 3 minutes until fish is lightly
coloured. Remove with a slotted spoon,
drain on kitchen paper and set aside.

Add remaining ingredients to the wok and
stir-fry for 2-3 minutes over a high heat until
thick and syrupy. Replace fish mixture and
cook for 2 minutes, stirring gently. Serve
immediately with noodles and salad.

Serves 4.

LIME GRILLED FISH SKEWERS

350 g (12 oz) monkfish tails, skinned and cut into
  2 cm (¾ in) cubes
350 g (12 oz) trout fillets, skinned and cut into 2 cm
  (¾ in) pieces
2 limes
1 teaspoon sesame oil
large pinch of five-spice powder
freshly ground black pepper
pared lime rind, to garnish

Place monkfish and trout in a shallow dish.
Juice one of the limes and grate the rind.
Mix with sesame oil and five-spice powder,
pour over fish, cover and chill for 30
minutes.

Soak 4 bamboo skewers in cold water. Halve
and quarter remaining lime lengthwise, and
then halve each quarter in the same way.
Slice each piece of lime in half widthwise to
make 16 small pieces.

Preheat grill (broiler). Thread monkfish,
trout and lime pieces on to skewers and place
on grill (broiler) rack. Brush with marinade
and season with black pepper. Grill (broil)
for 2 minutes on each side, brushing occasionally with marinade to prevent drying
out. Drain on kitchen paper, garnish with
lime rind and serve with rice, vegetables and
lime wedges.

Serves 4.

COD WITH OYSTER SAUCE

700 g (1½ lb) piece cod fillet, skinned
2 shallots, shredded
115 g (4 oz) oyster mushrooms, shredded
2 cloves garlic, finely sliced
115 g (4 oz) cooked, peeled prawns (shrimp),
   thawed and dried, if frozen
4 tablespoons oyster sauce
2 tablespoons dry sherry
salt and freshly ground black pepper
grated rind of 1 lime and 1 lemon
2 tablespoons chopped fresh coriander (cilantro)

Preheat oven to 180C (350F/Gas 4). Wash cod fillet and pat dry with kitchen paper. Place on a large piece of baking parchment and put in a roasting tin (pan). Top cod with shallots, mushrooms, garlic and prawns (shrimp) and spoon over oyster sauce and sherry. Season with salt and pepper.

Bring the ends of the baking parchment over the fish and pleat together to seal. Bake for 25 minutes or until cod is cooked through. Carefully lift from paper, sprinkle with lime and lemon rind and coriander (cilantro) and serve with rice and salad.

Serves 4.

COD WITH VINEGAR SAUCE

1 tablespoon sunflower oil
6 shallots, sliced
2 tablespoons white rice vinegar
2 teaspoons caster sugar
1 tablespoon light soy sauce
300 ml (10 fl oz/1¼ cups) Singaporean Vegetable
   Stock (see page 12)
1 teaspoon cornflour (cornstarch) mixed with 2
   teaspoons water
4 × 175 g (6 oz) cod steaks
salt and freshly ground black pepper
2 tablespoons chopped fresh chives

Heat half oil in a non-stick or well seasoned wok and stir-fry shallots for 2-3 minutes.

Add vinegar, sugar and soy sauce and stir-fry for 1 minute. Pour in stock and bring to the boil. Simmer for 8-9 minutes until thickened and slightly reduced. Stir in cornflour (cornstarch) mixture and cook, stirring, until thickened. Keep warm.

Preheat grill (broiler) or barbecue. Season cod steaks on both sides and place on grill (broiler) rack. Brush with remaining oil and cook for 4 minutes on each side until cooked through. Drain on kitchen paper. Remove skin. Stir chives into vinegar sauce, spoon over cod steaks and serve with noodles and grilled (broiled) tomatoes.

Serve 4.

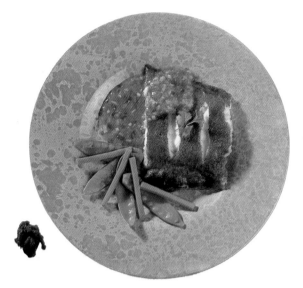

STEAMED FISH

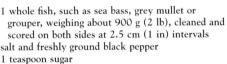

1 whole fish, such as sea bass, grey mullet or
  grouper, weighing about 900 g (2 lb), cleaned and
  scored on both sides at 2.5 cm (1 in) intervals
salt and freshly ground black pepper
1 teaspoon sugar
1 teaspoon chopped fresh root ginger
1 tablespoon each chopped white and green parts of
  spring onions (scallions)
1 tablespoon Thai fish sauce
2 teaspoons sesame oil
1 tablespoon shredded fresh root ginger
1 tablespoon vegetable oil
1 tablespoon each black bean sauce and soy sauce
2 small fresh red chillies, deseeded and shredded
fresh coriander (cilantro) sprigs, to garnish

Rub the fish inside and out with salt and
pepper, then marinate in a shallow dish with
the sugar, ginger, white parts of spring onions
(scallions), the fish sauce and sesame oil for
30 minutes. Place fish with marinade in a
hot steamer, or on a rack inside a wok, cover
and steam for 15-20 minutes.

Remove dish from the steamer or wok, place
the ginger and green part of spring onions
(scallions) on top of the fish. Heat vegetable
oil in a small saucepan, add black bean sauce,
soy sauce and chillies and stir-fry for 30
seconds, then drizzle it over fish. Garnish with
coriander and serve with rice and a salad.

Serves 4.

Note: If the fish is too big to fit into the
steamer or wok, cut it in half crossways and
re-assemble it on a warmed plate to serve.

GRILLED FLAT FISH

575 g (1¼ lb) flat fish, such as plaice or flounder,
  cleaned
salt and freshly ground black pepper
1 tablespoon vegetable oil, plus extra for brushing
½ teaspoon minced garlic
½ teaspoon chopped fresh root ginger
2 shallots, finely chopped
2-3 small fresh red chillies, deseeded and chopped
1 tablespoon chopped spring onion (scallion)
2 tablespoons Thai fish sauce and 1 teaspoon sugar
1 tablespoon tamarind water or lime juice
2-3 tablespoons chicken stock or water
2 teaspoons cornflour (cornstarch)

Score both sides of the fish at 2.5 cm (1 in)
intervals and rub with salt and pepper.

Leave the fish to stand for 25 minutes.
Meanwhile, preheat grill (broiler). Brush
both sides of fish with oil and grill (broil)
under the hot grill (broiler) for about 4
minutes each side until lightly brown but not
burnt. Place on a warmed serving dish.

Heat the 1 tablespoon oil in a small pan and
stir-fry the garlic, ginger, shallots, chillies
and spring onion for 1 minute, then add the
fish sauce, sugar, tamarind water or lime juice
and stock or water. Bring to boil and simmer
for 30 seconds. Mix cornflour (cornstarch)
with 1 tablespoon water and stir into sauce
to thicken. Pour the sauce over the fish.
Serve with carrots and mange tout (snow
peas), garnished with coriander (cilantro)
sprigs.

Serves 2 on its own, or 4-6 with other dishes as

FISH STIR-FRY WITH GINGER

55 g (2 oz/½ cup) cornflour (cornstarch)
½ teaspoon ground ginger
1 teaspoon ground sea salt
700 g (1½ lb) haddock or other firm white fish
    fillets, skinned and cubed
3 tablespoons peanut oil
2.5 cm (1 in) piece fresh root ginger, finely chopped
4 spring onions (scallions), thinly sliced
1 tablespoon ChingKiang vinegar or red wine vinegar
2 tablespoons rice wine or dry sherry
3 tablespoons dark soy sauce
1 teaspoon sugar
3 tablespoons fresh orange juice

FISH WITH CHILLI SAUCE

1 flat fish, such as pomfret, plump plaice or lemon
    sole, gutted and cleaned
vegetable oil for brushing
2 teaspoons vegetable oil
3 small dried red chillies, halved lengthwise
2 cloves garlic, finely chopped
1 teaspoon Thai fish sauce
75 ml (2½ fl oz/½ cup) tamarind water, see page 8-9
1 teaspoon crushed palm sugar

In a bowl, mix together cornflour (cornstarch), ground ginger and salt, add fish in batches to coat evenly.

Preheat grill (broiler). Brush fish lightly with oil, then grill (broil) for about 4 minutes a side until lightly coloured and flesh flakes when tested with the point of a knife. Using a fish slice, transfer to a warmed plate and keep warm.

In a wok, heat oil. Add fish and fry for 4 minutes, occasionally turning gently, until evenly browned. In a bowl, mix together remaining ingredients, stir into wok, reduce the heat so the liquid just simmers, cover and cook for 4 minutes.

Serves 4.

In a small saucepan, heat vegetable oil, add chillies and garlic and cook for 1 minute. Stir in remaining ingredients and simmer for 2-3 minutes until lightly thickened. Spoon over fish.

Serves 2.

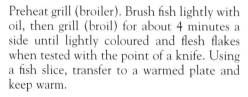

SEA TREASURES STIR-FRY

COCONUT CURRIED FISH

2 tablespoons cornflour (cornstarch)
1 egg white
175 g (6 oz) prepared raw prawns (shrimp)
175 g (6 oz) prepared squid
175 g (6 oz) shelled scallops, sliced
2 tablespoons peanut oil
1 carrot, thinly sliced
2 celery sticks, chopped
2.5 cm (1 in) piece fresh root ginger, finely chopped
3 cloves garlic, finely chopped
4 spring onions (scallions), finely chopped
115 ml (4 fl oz/½ cup) Singaporean Chicken Stock (see page 11)
1 teaspoon sea salt
1 tablespoon rice wine or dry sherry
1 teaspoon rice vinegar

6 cloves garlic, chopped
2.5 cm (1 in) piece fresh root ginger, chopped
1 large fresh red chilli, cored, deseeded and chopped
4 tablespoons vegetable oil
1 large onion, quartered and sliced
2 teaspoons ground cumin
½ teaspoon ground turmeric
400 ml (14 fl oz/1¾ cups) coconut milk
salt
450 g (1 lb) firm white fish fillet such as cod or halibut, cut into 5 cm (2 in) pieces
fresh coriander (cilantro) sprigs and lime wedges, to garnish

In a bowl mix together cornflour (cornstarch) and egg white to make a light batter. Separately, dip prawns (shrimp), squid and scallops into batter to coat evenly; allow excess batter to drain off. Reserve any remaining batter.

Put garlic, ginger and chilli in a blender. Add 150 ml (5 fl oz/⅔ cup) water. Mix until smooth.

In a wok or sauté pan over medium heat, heat oil. Add onion and fry 5-7 minutes until beginning to colour. Add cumin and turmeric and stir for 30 seconds. Stir in garlic mixture. Cook, stirring, for about 2 minutes until liquid has evaporated.

In a wok, heat oil, add prawns (shrimp), scallops, squid, celery and carrot, fry for about 3 minutes, then drain on kitchen paper. Pour oil from wok, leaving just 1 tablespoonful. Stir in remaining ingredients and bring to the boil. Reduce heat so sauce simmers, add seafood and vegetables and stir gently for 2 minutes. If sauce is thin, stir in 1 teaspoon reserved batter to thicken.

Pour coconut milk into pan. Bring to a boil and bubble until sauce is reduced by half. Add salt to taste. Add fish. Spoon sauce over fish so it is covered. Heat to a simmer and cook gently for 4-6 minutes until just flakes when tested with point of a sharp knife. Garnish with coriander (cilantro) sprigs and lime wedges. Serve with rice.

Serves 4.

Serves 3-4.

PRAWNS WITH GARLIC

PRAWNS IN COCONUT SAUCE

2 tablespoons vegetable oil
5 cloves garlic, chopped
5 mm (¼ in) slice fresh root ginger, very finely chopped
14-16 large prawns (shrimp), peeled, tails left on
2 teaspoons fish sauce
2 tablespoons chopped fresh coriander (cilantro) leaves
freshly ground black pepper
lettuce leaves, lime juice and diced cucumber, to serve

In a wok, heat oil, add garlic and fry until browned.

Stir in ginger, heat for 30 seconds, then add prawns (shrimp) and stir-fry for 2-3 minutes until beginning to turn opaque. Stir in fish sauce, coriander (cilantro), 1-2 tablespoons water and plenty of black pepper. Allow to bubble for 1-2 minutes.

Serve prawns on a bed of lettuce leaves with lime juice squeezed over and scattered with cucumber.

Serves 4.

2 fresh red chillies, deseeded and chopped
1 red onion, chopped
1 thick stalk lemon grass, chopped
2.5 cm (1 in) piece galangal, chopped
1 teaspoon ground turmeric
225 ml (8 fl oz/1 cup) coconut milk
14-16 raw Mediterranean (king) prawns (jumbo shrimp), peeled and deveined
8 fresh Thai holy basil leaves
2 teaspoons lime juice
1 teaspoon Thai fish sauce
1 spring onion (scallion), including some green, cut into fine strips

Using a small blender, mix chillies, onion, lemon grass and galangal to a paste. Transfer to a wok and heat, stirring, for 2-3 minutes. Stir in turmeric and 125 ml (4 fl oz/½ cup) water, bring to the boil and simmer for 3-4 minutes until most of the water has evaporated.

Stir in coconut milk and prawns and cook gently, stirring occasionally, for about 4 minutes until prawns (shrimp) are just firm and pink. Stir in basil leaves, lime juice and fish sauce. Scatter over strips of spring onion (scallion).

Serves 4.

FRAGRANT PRAWNS

2 dried shrimps
2 tablespoons vegetable oil
5 whole small fresh red chillies
1 small onion, finely chopped
3 cloves garlic, finely chopped
2.5 cm (1 in) piece fresh root ginger, grated
1 teaspoon curry powder
leaves from 2 stalks of fresh curry leaves
450 g (1 lb) raw unpeeled medium prawns (shrimp),
   peeled and deveined
1 tablespoon yellow bean sauce
1 teaspoon oyster sauce
1 teaspoon dark soy sauce
2 teaspoons rice wine
pinch sugar

Soak dried shrimps in hot water for 10 minutes. Drain and pound in a mortar or mix in a small blender. In a wok or sauté pan, heat oil over medium heat. Add chillies, onion, garlic and ginger. Fry for 1 minute. Add curry powder and curry leaves. Stir for 30 seconds.

Stir in prawns (shrimp) and dried shrimps then add yellow bean sauce, oyster sauce and soy sauce. Bring to a simmer, cover pan then cook gently for 2-3 minutes until prawns (shrimp) begin to turn pink. Add rice wine, and sugar to taste. Increase heat and stir for a few seconds. Serve immediately.

Serves 4.

PRAWNS ROBED IN SPICES

8 candlenuts or cashew nuts
2 teaspoons lime juice
2 large shallots, chopped
4 cloves garlic, crushed
2.5 cm (1 in) piece galangal, chopped
2.5 cm (1 in) piece fresh root ginger, chopped
1 stalk lemon grass, chopped
½ teaspoon ground turmeric
4 tablespoons vegetable oil
575 g (1¼ lb) raw unpeeled medium prawns
   (shrimp), peeled and deveined

Put nuts in a blender and grind to a powder. Transfer to a small bowl. Stir in lime juice and 1 tablespoon water. Set aside.

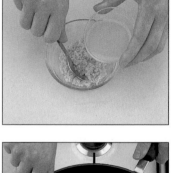

Put shallots, garlic, galangal, ginger, lemon grass and turmeric in blender. Add 2-3 tablespoons water and mix to a paste. In a wok or large non-stick frying pan (skillet) over medium heat, heat oil. Add spice paste and cook, stirring for about 5 minutes until reduced and reddish-brown in colour.

Add prawns (shrimp) and nut mixture. Increase heat to high and fry, stirring, for 2-3 minutes until prawns (shrimp) are cooked and spice mixture clings to them. Using a slotted spoon transfer to a warm plate, leaving all oil behind.

Serves 3-4

STIR-FRIED PRAWNS & GINGER

3 cloves garlic, crushed
4 cm (1½ in) piece fresh root ginger, thinly sliced
2 tablespoons vegetable oil
12-16 raw Mediterranean (king) prawns (jumbo shrimp), peeled and deveined
2 red shallots, finely chopped
grated rind ½ kaffir lime
2 teaspoons Thai fish sauce
3 spring onions (scallions), thinly sliced
lime juice, to serve

Using a pestle and mortar or small blender, pound or mix together garlic and ginger. In a wok, heat oil, add garlic paste and stir-fry for 2-3 minutes. Stir in prawns (shrimp) and shallots and stir-fry for 2 minutes.

Stir in lime rind, fish sauce and 3 tablespoons water. Allow to bubble for 1 minute until prawns (shrimp) become opaque and cooked through. Stir in spring onions (scallions), then remove from heat. Serve in a warmed dish, sprinkled with lime juice and garnished with spring onion (scallion) brushes.

Serves 3-4.

JACKETED PRAWNS

4 cm (1½ in) length cucumber
Dipping Sauce (see page 120)
8 raw Mediterranean (king) prawns (jumbo shrimp)
vegetable oil for deep frying
leaves from 1 coriander sprig, chopped
Batter:
115 g (4 oz/⅔ cup) rice flour
3 tablespoons desiccated (unsweetened shredded) coconut
1 egg, separated
175 ml (6 fl oz/¾ cup) coconut milk
1 teaspoon Thai fish sauce

Cut cucumber into quarters lengthwise, remove and discard seeds, then thickly slice. Place in a small bowl and add dipping sauce. Set aside. Peel prawns (shrimp), leaving tails on. Cut along back of each one and remove black spinal cord. Set prawns (shrimp) aside. In a wok, heat oil to 180C (350F).

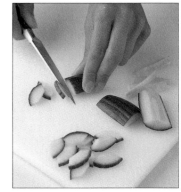

For batter, in a bowl, stir together flour and coconut. Gradually stir in egg yolk, coconut milk and fish sauce. In a bowl, whisk egg white until stiff; fold into batter. Dip prawns (shrimp) in batter to coat evenly. Deep fry in batches for 2-3 minutes until golden. Using a slotted spoon, transfer to kitchen paper. Keep warm while frying remainder. Add coriander (cilantro) to sauce and serve with prawns (shrimp).

Serves 3-4.

STEAMED PRAWNS & MUSHROOMS

1 dried red chilli, deseeded, soaked in hot water for
  20 minutes, drained and chopped
3 cm (1¼ in) piece fresh root ginger, chopped
2 cloves garlic, chopped
2 shallots, chopped
1 stalk lemon grass, chopped
1 tablespoon Thai fish sauce
15-20 fresh Thai holy basil leaves
16 raw Mediterranean (king) prawns (jumbo
  shrimp), peeled with tails left intact, deveined
2-3 large shiitake mushrooms, thinly sliced

Using a pestle and mortar or small blender,
pound or mix together chilli, ginger, garlic,
shallots and lemon grass. Stir in fish sauce
and basil leaves.

Place prawns (shrimp) in a shallow heatproof bowl and spoon spice mixture over to
coat evenly. Add mushrooms. Alternatively,
wrap prawns (shrimp) and mushrooms in a
banana leaf and secure with wooden cocktail
sticks (toothpicks). Place bowl or banana
leaf parcel in a steamer above boiling water.
Cover and cook for 8 minutes until prawns
(shrimp) are tender.

Serves 3-4

PRAWNS WITH LEMON GRASS

2 cloves garlic, chopped
1 tablespoon chopped fresh coriander (cilantro)
2 tablespoons chopped lemon grass
½ teaspoon black or white peppercorns
3 tablespoons vegetable oil
350-400 g (12-14 oz) raw peeled prawns (shrimp),
  cut in half lengthwise if large
2 shallots or 1 small onion, sliced
2-3 small fresh chillies, deseeded and chopped
2-3 tomatoes, cut into wedges
1 tablespoon Thai fish sauce
1 tablespoon oyster sauce
2-3 tablespoons chicken stock or water
fresh coriander (cilantro) sprigs, to garnish

Using a pestle and mortar, pound the garlic,
coriander (cilantro), lemon grass and peppercorns to a paste. Heat oil in a wok or frying pan (skillet) and stir-fry the spicy paste
for 15-20 seconds until fragrant. Add prawns
(shrimp), shallots or onion, chillies and
tomatoes and stir-fry for 2-3 minutes.

Add fish sauce, oyster sauce and stock, bring
to the boil and simmer for 2-3 minutes.
Serve garnished with coriander (cilantro)
sprigs.

Serves 4.

STIR-FRIED SCALLOPS

450 g (1 lb) fresh queen (bay) scallops, cleaned and
    trimmed
225 g (8 oz) baby sweetcorn
225 g (8 oz) mange tout (snow peas)
1 tablespoon sunflower oil
2 shallots, chopped
1 clove garlic, finely chopped
1 cm (½ in) piece fresh root ginger, finely chopped
2 tablespoons yellow bean sauce
1 tablespoon light soy sauce
1 teaspoon caster sugar
1 tablespoon dry sherry

Wash scallops and dry with kitchen paper.
Slice the baby sweetcorn in half lengthwise
and top and tail the mange tout (snow peas).
Heat the oil in a non-stick or well seasoned
wok and stir-fry the shallots, garlic and ginger for 1 minute.

Add scallops, baby sweetcorn and mange
tout (snow peas) and stir-fry for 1 minute.
Stir in remaining ingredients and simmer for
4 minutes or until scallops and vegetables are
cooked through.

Serves 4.

STIR-FRIED PRAWNS

300 g (10 oz) raw peeled prawns (shrimp)
3 tablespoons vegetable oil
1 teaspoon chopped garlic
½ teaspoon chopped fresh root ginger
1 tablespoon chopped spring onion (scallion)
115 g (4 oz) straw mushrooms, halved lengthwise
55 g (2 oz) water chestnuts, sliced
3 tablespoons Thai fish sauce
1 tablespoon sugar
about 2-3 tablespoons chicken stock or water
1 teaspoon chilli sauce (optional)
salt and freshly ground black pepper
fresh coriander (cilantro) sprigs, to garnish

Halve prawns (shrimp) lengthwise. Heat oil
in a wok or pan and stir-fry the garlic, ginger
and spring onion (scallion) for about 20 seconds. Add the prawns (shrimp), mushrooms
and water chestnuts and stir-fry for about 2
minutes.

Add fish sauce and sugar, stir for a few times,
then add stock or water. Bring to the boil
and stir for another minute or so. Finally, add
the chilli sauce, if using, and season with salt
and pepper. Garnish with coriander
(cilantro) sprigs and serve at once.

Serves 4.

Variation: This is a standard stir-fry recipe. If
preferred, use different types of fish or meat,
cut into small, thin slices, and cook with any
other kind of vegetables.

SCALLOPS WITH VEGETABLES

3 tablespoons vegetable oil
1 teaspoon chopped garlic
1-2 small red chillies, deseeded and chopped
2 shallots or 1 small onion, chopped
55 g (2 oz) mange tout (snow peas)
1 small carrot, thinly sliced
225 g (8 oz) fresh scallops, sliced
55 g (2 oz) sliced bamboo shoots
2 tablespoons black mushrooms, soaked and sliced
2-3 spring onions (scallions), cut into short sections
2 tablespoons Thai fish sauce
1 teaspoon sugar
about 2-3 tablespoons chicken stock or water
1 tablespoon oyster sauce
salt and freshly ground black pepper
fresh coriander (cilantro) sprigs, to garnish

Heat oil in a wok or pan and stir-fry garlic, chillies and shallots or onion for about 20 seconds. Add the mange tout (snow peas) and carrot and stir-fry for about 2 minutes. Add scallops, bamboo shoots, dried mushrooms and spring onions (scallions) and stir-fry for 1 minute.

Add fish sauce and sugar, blend well and stir for 1 more minute, then add the stock or water. Bring to the boil and stir for a few more seconds. Add oyster sauce and season with salt and pepper. Garnish with coriander (cilantro) sprigs and serve at once.

Serves 4.

SCALLOPS WITH LIME

12 scallops on the half shell
1 tablespoon vegetable oil
2 cloves garlic, chopped
1 red shallot, finely chopped
5 mm (¼ in) slice galangal, finely chopped
freshly ground black pepper
1 teaspoon finely chopped fresh red chilli
3 tablespoons lime juice
¼ teaspoon crushed palm sugar
1 teaspoon Thai fish sauce
shredded fresh coriander (cilantro) leaves, to garnish

Lay scallops on their shells in a steaming basket.

In a wok, heat oil, add garlic and shallot and cook, stirring occasionally, until softened. Add galangal and stir for 1 minute. Sprinkle over scallops and grind over black pepper. Cover steaming basket and place over a wok or saucepan of boiling water. Steam for 6-8 minutes until scallops just begin to turn opaque.

In a saucepan, gently heat chilli, lime juice, sugar and fish sauce until sugar dissolves. Transfer scallops on their shells to a warmed serving plate, spoon over lime sauce and scatter with coriander (cilantro).

Serves 3-4.

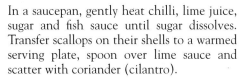

CURRIED CRAB

700 g (1½ lb) cooked large crab claws, thawed and
   dried, if frozen
1 tablespoon sunflower oil
2 cloves garlic, thinly sliced
1 large green pepper (capsicum), shredded
225 g (8 oz) small broccoli flowerets
5 tablespoons Singaporean Vegetable Stock, page 12
1 tablespoon Madras curry paste
1 tablespoon light soy sauce
1 teaspoon brown sugar
lemon wedges, to serve

Wrap the end of a rolling pin in cling film
and tap the main part of the crab claws until
the shell cracks, leaving pincers intact. Peel
away hard shell to expose crab flesh, leaving
shell on pincers. Heat oil in a non-stick or
well seasoned wok and stir-fry crab and garlic for 1-2 minutes until crab is lightly
browned. Drain on kitchen paper and set
aside.

Mix together remaining ingredients and add
to wok. Simmer gently for 5 minutes, stirring
occasionally. Replace crab and garlic and
cook gently for 2-3 minutes, stirring to coat
crab with sauce. Serve immediately with
rice, vegetables and lemon wedges.

Serves 4.

MUSSELS IN HOT SPICY SAUCE

4 dried red chillies, deseeded
2 teaspoons shrimp paste, roasted (see page 8-9)
1 small onion, chopped
2.5 cm (1 in) piece fresh galangal
4 cloves garlic, 3 coarsely chopped and 1 finely
   chopped
1 lemon grass stalk, sliced
6-8 candlenuts or cashew nuts
1 teaspoon paprika
4 tablespoons vegetable oil
900 g-1.35 kg (2-3 lb) live mussels, cleaned

Put chillies in a small bowl. Add 4 tablespoons hot water and soak until slightly softened. Pour into a blender.

Add shrimp paste, onion, galangal, coarsely
chopped garlic, lemon grass, nuts and
paprika. Mix to a paste, adding a little extra
water if necessary. In a wok or large sauté
pan, heat oil over medium-high heat. Add
finely chopped garlic and stir until just
beginning to brown. Add spice paste and stir
for 3 minutes.

Pour in 350 ml (12 fl oz/1½ cups) water and
bring to a boil. Add all the mussels. Return
quickly to boil then cover pan and cook over
medium-high heat for 3-5 minutes, shaking
and tossing pan halfway through, until all
mussels have opened; discard any mussels
that remain closed. Serve mussels in deep
bowls with cooking juices spooned over.

Serves 2-4.

SPICY CRAB

1 clove garlic, chopped
2 shallots or the white parts of 3-4 spring onions
  (scallions), chopped
1 teaspoon chopped fresh root ginger
1 tablespoon chopped lemon grass
2-3 tablespoons vegetable oil
1 teaspoon chilli sauce
1 tablespoon sugar
3-4 tablespoons coconut milk
about 450 ml (16 fl oz/2 cups) chicken stock
3 tablespoons Thai fish sauce
2 tablespoons lime juice or vinegar
meat from 1 large or 2 medium cooked crabs, cut
  into small pieces
salt and freshly ground black pepper
fresh coriander (cilantro) sprigs, to garnish

Using a pestle and mortar, pound the garlic, shallots or spring onions (scallions), ginger, and lemon grass to a fine paste. Heat oil in clay pot or flameproof casserole, add the garlic mixture, chilli sauce and sugar and stir-fry for about 1 minute. Add the coconut milk, stock, fish sauce and lime juice or vinegar and bring to the boil.

Add the crab pieces and season with salt and pepper. Blend well and cook for 3-4 minutes, stirring constantly, then serve hot, garnished with coriander (cilantro) sprigs.

Serves 4.

Note: Uncooked crabs can be used for this dish, but increase the cooking time by about 8-10 minutes.

MUSSELS WITH BASIL

700 g (1½ lb) fresh mussels in shell, cleaned,
  bearded and rinsed
1 large clove garlic, chopped
7.5 cm (3 in) piece galangal, thickly sliced
2 stalks lemon grass, chopped
10 fresh Thai holy basil sprigs
1 tablespoon Thai fish sauce
fresh Thai holy basil leaves, to garnish
Dipping Sauce (see page 120), to serve

Place mussels, garlic, galangal, lemon grass, basil sprigs and fish sauce in a large saucepan. Add water to a depth of 1 cm (½ in), cover pan, bring to the boil and cook for about 5 minutes, shaking pan frequently, until mussels have opened; discard any that remain closed.

Transfer mussels to a large warmed bowl, or individual bowls, and strain over cooking liquid. Scatter over basil leaves. Serve with sauce to dip mussels into.

Serves 2-3.

POULTRY DISHES

CHICKEN WINGS IN SPICY SAUCE

GINGER CHICKEN PATTIES

8-12 chicken wings
salt and freshly ground black pepper
1 tablespoon sugar
1 tablespoon Thai fish sauce
oil for deep-frying
250 ml (9 fl oz/1 cup) Hot Sauce, page 119
about 85 ml (3 fl oz/⅓ cup) chicken stock or water
1 tablespoon clear honey
lettuce leaves, to serve

Trim off tip of each chicken wing (these are known as pinions), which can be used for stock making.

450 g (1 lb) lean chicken, minced (ground)
1 clove garlic, finely chopped
2.5 cm (1 in) piece fresh root ginger, peeled and finely chopped
4 tablespoons chopped fresh coriander (cilantro)
1 tablespoon cornflour (cornstarch)
225 g (8 oz/2 cups) cooked long grain white rice
salt and freshly ground black pepper
1 egg white, lightly beaten
2 teaspoons sunflower oil
fresh coriander (cilantro) leaves, to garnish
DIP:
2 tablespoons light soy sauce
2 tablespoons dry sherry
1 cm (½ in) piece fresh root ginger, peeled and grated

In a bowl, marinate the chicken wings with salt, pepper, sugar and fish for at least 30 minutes, longer if possible. Heat oil in a wok or deep-fat fryer to 160C (325F) and deep-fry the chicken wings for 2-3 minutes until golden; remove and drain.

In a bowl, mix together the minced (ground) chicken, garlic, ginger and coriander (cilantro). Stir in the cornflour (cornstarch), cooked rice and seasoning. Bind together with egg white. Divide the mixture into 8 portions and shape into 7.5 cm (3 in) diameter patties, dusting the hands with extra cornflour (cornstarch) if needed. Place on a plate, cover and chill for 30 minutes.

Heat the hot sauce with chicken stock or water in a saucepan and add the chicken wings. Bring to the boil and braise for 5-6 minutes, stirring constantly until the sauce is sticky. Add the honey and blend well. Serve hot or cold on a bed of lettuce leaves.

Serves 4-6

Preheat grill (broiler). Brush grill rack lightly with oil and place patties on rack. Brush tops lightly with oil and cook for 4 minutes. Turn patties over, brush again with oil and cook for a further 3–4 minutes until cooked through. Drain on kitchen paper. Mix together ingredients for dip. Garnish patties with coriander (cilantro) and serve with the dip and salad.

Serves 4.

CHICKEN WITH MUSHROOMS

LEMON & HONEY CHICKEN

450 g (1 lb) skinless, boneless chicken thighs
1 tablespoon sunflower oil
225 g (8 oz) button mushrooms, sliced
225 g (8 oz) spring onions (scallions), chopped
1 clove garlic, finely chopped
2.5 cm (1 in) piece fresh root ginger, finely chopped
150 ml (5 fl oz/⅔ cup) Singaporean Chicken Stock, page 11
2 tablespoons rice wine
2 tablespoons dark soy sauce
2 tablespoons oyster sauce
425 g (15 oz) can straw mushrooms, drained
1 teaspoon cornflour (cornstarch) mixed with 2 teaspoons water

4 × 115 g (4 oz) boneless chicken breasts
3 tablespoons clear honey
4 teaspoons light soy sauce
grated rind and juice of 2 lemons
1 clove garlic, finely chopped
freshly ground black pepper
1 tablespoon sunflower oil
2 tablespoons chopped fresh chives
thin strips of lemon rind, to garnish

Skin and trim the chicken breasts. Using a sharp knife, score the chicken breasts in a criss-cross pattern on both sides, taking care not to slice all the way through. Place in a shallow dish.

Trim the chicken thighs. Cut into 2.5 cm (1 in) strips. Heat the oil in a non-stick or well seasoned wok and stir-fry the chicken strips for 3-4 minutes until chicken is lightly browned all over.

Mix together the honey, soy sauce, lemon rind and juice, garlic and black pepper. Pour over chicken, cover and chill for 1 hour.

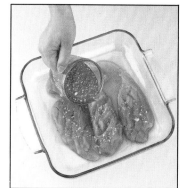

Add sliced mushrooms, spring onions (scallions), garlic and ginger and stir-fry for 2 minutes. Stir in remaining ingredients and simmer gently, stirring, for 5 minutes. Serve with noodles.

Serves 4.

Heat the oil in a non-stick or well seasoned wok. Drain chicken, reserving marinade, and cook for 2-3 minutes on each side, until lightly golden. Add marinade and simmer gently for 5 minutes, turning frequently, until chicken is cooked through and sauce syrupy. Stir in chives and garnish with lemon rind and serve on a bed of noodles.

Serves 4.

CHICKEN & BASIL STIR-FRY

450 g (1 lb) boneless chicken thighs
1 tablespoon dark soy sauce
1 tablespoon cornflour (cornstarch)
1 tablespoon groundnut (peanut) oil
2 cloves garlic, thinly sliced
1 fresh red chilli, deseeded and thinly sliced
1 teaspoon chilli powder
1 tablespoon hoisin sauce
small bunch fresh basil leaves, shredded
fresh basil leaves and blanched red chilli strips, to
    garnish

Skin and trim the chicken. Cut into 2.5 cm
(1 in) strips and place in a bowl. Stir in the
soy sauce and cornflour (cornstarch).

Heat the oil in a non-stick or well seasoned
wok and stir-fry chicken with garlic and
chilli for 7-8 minutes.

Add chilli powder and hoisin sauce and cook
for a further 2 minutes. Remove from heat
and stir in shredded basil. Garnish with basil
and chilli strips and serve on a bed of rice.

Serves 4.

CHICKEN & PLUM CASSEROLE

25 g (1 oz) dried Chinese mushrooms, soaked in hot
    water for 20 minutes
450 g (1 lb) skinless, boneless chicken thighs
1 tablespoon sunflower oil
2 cloves garlic, thinly sliced
25 g (1 oz) Parma ham, trimmed and diced
225 g (8 oz) plums, halved and stoned (pitted)
1 tablespoon brown sugar
3 tablespoons light soy sauce
2 tablespoons rice wine
3 tablespoons plum sauce
1 tablespoon chilli sauce
550 ml (20 fl oz/2½ cups) Singaporean Chicken
    Stock, page 11
2 teaspoons cornflour (cornstarch) mixed with 4
    teaspoons water

Drain mushrooms and squeeze out excess
water. Discard mushroom stalks and thinly
slice caps. Trim chicken thighs and cut into
2.5 cm (1 in) strips. Heat oil in a non-stick
or well seasoned wok and stir-fry chicken,
garlic and ham for 3-4 minutes. Add mushrooms and stir-fry for 1 minute.

Add remaining ingredients except cornflour
mixture and simmer for 20 minutes until the
plums have softened. Add cornflour (cornstarch) mixture, and cook, stirring, until
thickened. Serve on a bed of rice.

Serves 4.

CHICKEN WITH PEANUTS

450 g (1 lb) boneless chicken breasts
1 tablespoon chilli oil
2.5 cm (1 in) piece fresh root ginger, finely chopped
55 g (2 oz) raw peanuts, skins removed
1 tablespoon Singaporean Chicken Stock, page 11
1 tablespoon dry sherry
1 tablespoon dark soy sauce
1 teaspoon brown sugar
1 teaspoon five-spice powder
1 teaspoon white rice vinegar
4 spring onions (scallions), finely chopped

Skin and trim the chicken breasts. Cut into 2.5 cm (1 in) pieces.

Heat the oil in a non-stick or well seasoned wok and gently stir-fry the chicken, ginger and peanuts for 2 minutes until the chicken is just coloured.

Add the remaining ingredients except the spring onions and simmer for 5 minutes, stirring occasionally. Remove from heat and stir in spring onions. Serve with salad.

Serves 4.

CHICKEN WITH CUCUMBER

225 g (8 oz) cucumber
2 teaspoons salt
450 g (1 lb) boneless chicken breasts
1 tablespoon groundnut (peanut) oil
2 cloves garlic, finely chopped
1 tablespoon light soy sauce
1 tablespoon dry sherry
2 tablespoons chopped fresh chives
cucumber twists, to garnish

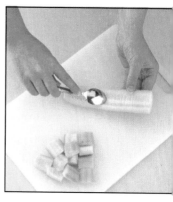

Peel the cucumber, halve lengthwise and scoop out the seeds with a teaspoon. Cut into 2.5 cm (1 in) cubes, place in a bowl and sprinkle with salt. Set aside for 20 minutes.

Skin and trim chicken. Cut into 1 cm (½ in) strips. Drain cucumber and rinse well. Pat dry with kitchen paper.

Heat oil in a non-stick or well seasoned wok and stir-fry the chicken and garlic for 5 minutes. Add soy sauce, sherry, chives and cucumber and cook for 3 minutes. Garnish with cucumber twists.

Serves 4.

CHICKEN WITH MANGE TOUT

3 tablespoons vegetable oil
3 cloves garlic, chopped
1 dried red chilli, deseeded and chopped
3 red shallots, chopped
2 tablespoons lime juice
2 teaspoons fish sauce
350 g (12 oz) chicken, finely chopped
1½ stalks lemon grass, chopped
1 kaffir lime leaf, sliced
175 g (6 oz) mange tout (snow peas)
1½ tablespoons coarsely ground browned rice, see page 8-9
3 spring onions (scallions), chopped
chopped fresh coriander (cilantro) leaves, to garnish

In a wok, heat 2 tablespoons oil, add garlic and cook, stirring occasionally, until lightly browned. Stir in chilli, shallots, lime juice, fish sauce and 4 tablespoons water. Simmer for 1-2 minutes, then stir in chicken, lemon grass and lime leaf. Cook, stirring, for 2-3 until chicken is just cooked through. Transfer to a warmed plate and keep warm.

Heat remaining oil in wok, add mange tout (snow peas) and stir-fry for 2-3 minutes until just tender. Transfer to a warmed serving plate. Return chicken to wok. Add rice and spring onions (scallions). Heat for about 1 minute, then transfer to serving plate. Garnish with chopped coriander (cilantro).

Serves 3-4.

STEAMED CHICKEN CURRY

4 tablespoons Thai red curry paste
375 ml (13 fl oz/1⅔ cups) coconut milk
450 g (1 lb) chicken breast meat, sliced
4 kaffir lime leaves, shredded
8 fresh Thai holy basil leaves
fresh Thai holy basil sprig, to garnish

Using a small blender, mix together curry paste, 85 ml (3 fl oz/⅓ cup) coconut milk and 5 tablespoons water; set aside. Place chicken in a heatproof bowl or dish, stir in remaining coconut milk and set aside for 30 minutes.

Stir curry-flavoured coconut milk, lime leaves and basil leaves into bowl or dish. Cover top tightly with foil and place in a steaming basket.

Cover with a lid. Position over a saucepan of boiling water. Steam for about 40 minutes until chicken is tender. Garnish with basil.

Serves 4-5.

CHICKEN WITH LEMON GRASS

1.35 kg (3 lb) chicken, cut into 8 pieces
4 thick stalks lemon grass
4 spring onions (scallions), chopped
4 black peppercorns, cracked
2 tablespoons vegetable oil
1 fresh green chilli, deseeded and thinly sliced
2 teaspoons Thai fish sauce
fresh red chilli, cut into thin slivers, to garnish

With the point of a sharp knife, cut slashes in each chicken piece; place in a shallow dish.

Bruise top parts of each lemon grass stalk and reserve. Chop lower parts, then pound with spring onions (scallions) and peppercorns using a pestle and mortar. Spread over chicken and into slashes. Cover and set aside for 2 hours.

In a wok, heat oil, add chicken and cook, turning occasionally, for about 5 minutes until lightly browned. Add green chilli, bruised lemon grass stalks and 4 tablespoons water. Cover wok and cook slowly for 25-30 minutes until chicken is cooked through. Stir in fish sauce. Transfer chicken pieces to a warmed serving dish, spoon over cooking juices and sprinkle with red chilli.

Serves 4-6.

BARBECUED CHICKEN

4 fresh red chillies, seeded and sliced
2 cloves garlic, chopped
5 shallots, finely sliced
2 teaspoons crushed palm sugar
115 ml (4 fl oz/½ cup) coconut cream, see page 8-9
2 teaspoons Thai fish sauce
1 tablespoon tamarind water, see page 8-9
4 boneless chicken breasts
fresh Thai holy basil leaves or coriander (cilantro) leaves, to garnish

Using a pestle and mortar or small blender, pound chillies, garlic and shallots to a paste. Work in sugar, then stir in coconut cream, fish sauce and tamarind water.

Using the point of a sharp knife, cut 4 slashes in chicken breast. Place chicken in a shallow dish and pour over spice mixture. Turn to coat, cover dish and set aside for 1 hour.

Preheat grill (broiler). Place chicken on a piece of foil and grill (broil) for about 4 minutes a side, basting occasionally, until cooked through. Garnish with basil or coriander (cilantro) leaves.

Serves 4.

CHICKEN WITH GALANGAL

CHICKEN WITH PEANUT SAUCE

450 g (1 lb) chicken breast meat
3 tablespoons vegetable oil
2 cloves garlic, finely chopped
1 onion, quartered and sliced
2.5 cm (1 in) piece galangal, finely chopped
8 pieces dried Chinese black mushrooms, soaked for
  30 minutes, drained and chopped
1 fresh red chilli, deseeded and cut into fine strips
1 tablespoon Thai fish sauce
1½ teaspoons crushed palm sugar
1 tablespoon lime juice
12 fresh Thai mint leaves
4 spring onions (scallions), including some green,
  chopped
fresh Thai mint leaves, to garnish

2.5 cm (1 in) piece galangal, chopped
2 cloves garlic, chopped
1½ tablespoons red curry paste
4 tablespoons coconut cream, see page 8-9
450 g (1 lb) chicken breast meat, cut into large
  pieces
3 shallots, chopped
4 tablespoons dry-roasted peanuts, chopped
225 ml (8 fl oz/1 cup) coconut milk
½ teaspoon finely chopped dried red chilli
2 teaspoons fish sauce
freshly cooked broccoli, to serve

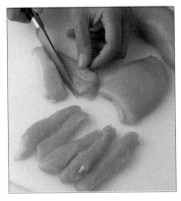

Using a sharp knife, cut chicken into 5.5 cm (2¼ in) long, 2.5 cm (1 in) wide pieces; set aside. In a wok, heat oil, add garlic and onion and cook, stirring occasionally, until golden. Stir in chicken and stir-fry for about 2 minutes.

Using a pestle and mortar or small blender, pound or mix together galangal, garlic and curry paste. Mix in coconut cream. Place chicken in a bowl and stir in spice mixture; set aside for 1 hour.

Add galangal, mushrooms and chilli and stir-fry for 1 minute. Stir in fish sauce, sugar, lime juice, mint leaves, spring onions (scallions) and 3-4 tablespoons water. Cook, stirring for about 1 minute. Transfer to a warmed serving dish and scatter over mint leaves.

Serves 4.

Heat a wok, add shallots and coated chicken and stir-fry for 3-4 minutes. In a blender, mix peanuts with coconut milk, then stir into chicken with chilli and fish sauce. Cook gently for about 30 minutes until chicken is tender and thick sauce formed. Transfer to centre of a warmed serving plate and arrange cooked broccoli around.

Serves 4.

LEMON GRASS CURRY CHICKEN

350 g (12 oz) boneless chicken, chopped into small
    pieces
1 tablespoon Thai red curry paste
3 tablespoons vegetable oil
2 cloves garlic, finely chopped
1 tablespoon Thai fish sauce
2 stalks lemon grass, finely chopped
5 kaffir lime leaves, shredded
½ teaspoon crushed palm sugar

Place chicken in a bowl, add curry paste and
stir to coat chicken; set aside for 30 minutes.

In a wok, heat oil, add garlic and fry until
golden. Stir in chicken, then fish sauce,
lemon grass, lime leaves, sugar and 115 ml
(4 fl oz/½ cup) water.

Adjust heat so liquid is barely moving and
cook for 15-20 minutes until chicken is
cooked through. If chicken becomes too dry,
add a little more water, but the final dish
should be quite dry.

Serves 3-4.

STIR-FRIED CHICKEN

225 g (8 oz) chicken fillet, boned and skinned
2 teaspoons cornflour (cornstarch)
2 teaspoons fish sauce
salt and freshly ground black pepper
2-3 tablespoons vegetable oil
½ teaspoon finely chopped garlic
1 teaspoon finely chopped lemon grass
1 teaspoon chopped fresh root ginger
4-6 dried small red chillies
55 g (2 oz) mange-tout (snow peas)
½ red pepper (capsicum), cut into cubes
55 g (2 oz) sliced bamboo shoots, drained
1 teaspoon sugar
1 tablespoon rice vinegar
2 tablespoons oyster sauce
½ teaspoon sesame oil

Cut chicken into bite-size slices or cubes.
Mix cornflour (cornstarch) with 1 tablespoon water. Place chicken in a bowl with
cornflour (cornstarch) paste and fish sauce.
Season with salt and pepper and leave to
marinate for 20-25 minutes. Heat oil in a
wok or frying pan (skillet) and stir-fry the
garlic, lemon grass, ginger and chillies for
about 30 seconds. Add the chicken pieces
and stir-fry for about 1 minute until the
colour of the chicken changes.

Add vegetables and cook for 2-3 minutes,
stirring constantly, then add sugar, vinegar,
oyster sauce and 3-4 tablespoons water.
Blend well, bring to boil and add the sesame
oil. Serve at once with flat rice noodles.

Serves 4.

Variation: Use chicken stock instead of the
3-4 tablespoons water.

CHICKEN IN SPICED SAUCE

2 tablespoons vegetable oil
6 each chicken thighs and drumsticks
2 lemon grass stalks, chopped
4 shallots, chopped
4 cloves garlic, chopped
7 cm (2½ in) piece of fresh root ginger, chopped
3 tablespoons ground coriander
2 teaspoons ground turmeric
4 fresh bay leaves
350 ml (12 fl oz/1½ cups) coconut milk
4 tablespoons Chinese chilli sauce
about 2 tablespoons brown sugar, or to taste
55 g (2 oz/½ cup) roasted candlenuts or cashew
  nuts, finely chopped
salt

In a large frying pan (skillet) over medium heat, heat oil. Add chicken and brown evenly. Transfer to paper towels to drain. Pour all but 1½ tablespoons fat from pan. Put lemon grass, shallots, garlic and ginger in a blender. Mix to a paste. Gently heat pan of fat, add spice paste and stir for 2 minutes. Stir in coriander, turmeric and bay leaves for 1 minute. Stir in coconut milk, chilli sauce, sugar, nuts and salt for a further minute.

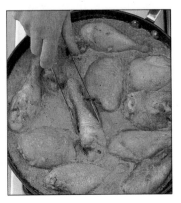

Return chicken to pan and turn in sauce. Cover and cook gently for 20 minutes, stirring and turning chicken frequently, until chicken juices run clear. Discard bay leaves before serving.

Serves 6.

SPICED CHICKEN

5 shallots, chopped
3 cloves garlic, chopped
5 coriander roots, chopped
2 stalks lemon grass, chopped
2 fresh red chillies, deseeded and chopped
4 cm (1½ in) piece fresh root ginger, finely chopped
1 teaspoon shrimp paste
1½ tablespoons vegetable oil
2 chicken legs, divided into thighs and drumsticks
1½ tablespoons tamarind water, see page 8-9

Using a pestle and mortar or small blender, pound or mix until smooth shallots, garlic, coriander, lemon grass, chillies, ginger and shrimp paste.

In a wok, heat oil, stir in spicy paste and cook, stirring, for 3-4 minutes. Stir in chicken pieces to coat evenly.

Add tamarind water and 85 ml (3 fl oz/ ⅓ cup) water. Cover and cook gently for about 25 minutes until chicken is tender. Garnish with coriander (cilantro) sprig.

Serves 3-4.

BRAISED CHICKEN WITH SPICES

CHICKEN & PINEAPPLE CURRY

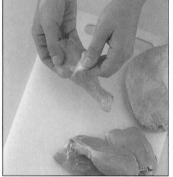

4 each chicken thighs and drumsticks, total weight
  about 1 kg (2¼ lb)
4 cloves garlic, chopped
2 shallots, chopped
5 cm (2 in) piece fresh root ginger, chopped
400 ml (14 fl oz/1¼ cups) coconut milk
2 teaspoons each ground coriander and ground
  cumin
¼ teaspoon ground turmeric
2 tablespoons vegetable oil
6 green cardamom pods
6 each star anise and dried red chillies
1 cinnamon stick
4 cloves
20 fresh curry leaves

5 shallots, chopped
3 large fresh red chillies, cored, seeded and chopped
3 cloves garlic, crushed
5 cm (2 in) piece galangal, chopped
1 stalk lemon grass, chopped
2 tablespoons vegetable oil
700 g (1½ lb) boneless, skinless chicken breast, cut
  into strips
2 tablespoons light brown sugar
2 × 400 ml (14 fl oz/1¼ cups) cans coconut milk
2 teaspoons tamarind paste (see page 8-9)
2 tablespoons Thai fish sauce
4 kaffir lime leaves
1 small pineapple, about 450 g (1 lb), thinly sliced
grated rind and juice of 1 lime, or to taste
small handful fresh coriander (cilantro) leaves, chopped

Skin chicken pieces and set aside. Put garlic,
shallots, ginger, coconut milk, coriander,
cumin and turmeric into a small blender.
Mix to a fine purée. In a heavy-based
saucepan large enough to hold chicken in a
single layer, heat oil over medium heat. Add
cardamom pods, star anise, chillies, cinnamon, cloves and curry leaves. Fry, stirring,
for 2-3 minutes. Add ⅓ of the coconut milk
mixture. Bring to boil then add chicken.
Turn to coat then cook for 5 minutes.

Put shallots, chillies, garlic, galangal and
lemon grass in a small blender. Mix to a
paste; add 1 tablespoon of the oil, if necessary. In a wok or sauté pan, heat remaining
oil. Add chicken and stir-fry until just turning pale golden brown. Remove and set
aside.

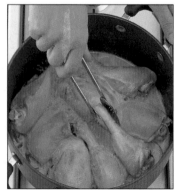

Add remaining coconut milk mixture. Bring
to a simmer then lower heat and cook gently,
uncovered, for 50 minutes, stirring frequently. Cook for a further 10 minutes, stirring every minute. The chicken should be
golden brown and most of the milk evaporated. Pour away oily residue. Increase heat
to high. Add 3-4 tablespoons water and stir
to deglaze pan. Serve chicken with Thai rice
and sauce.

Stir chilli paste into pan and stir-fry for 3-4
minutes until fragrant. Stir in sugar, coconut
milk, tamarind, fish sauce and kaffir lime
leaves. Bring to a boil, and boil for 4-5
minutes until reduced by half and lightly
thickened. Return chicken to pan. Add
pineapple and simmer for 3-4 minutes until
chicken juices run clear. Add the lime rind,
and lime juice to taste. Stir in coriander
(cilantro).

Serves 4.

Serves 6.

DEVIL'S CURRY

6 tablespoons vegetable oil
6 shallots, thinly sliced
3 cloves garlic, thinly sliced
1 teaspoon black mustard seeds, lightly crushed
1.5 kg (3½ lb) chicken, jointed, or small chicken portions
300 g (10 oz) small potatoes, halved
2 teaspoons mustard powder
2 tablespoons rice vinegar
1 tablespoon dark soy sauce
Spice paste:
10 fresh red chillies, cored, deseeded and chopped
5 cm (2 in) piece fresh root ginger, chopped
6 shallots, chopped
3 cloves garlic, chopped
1 tablespoon ground coriander
½ teaspoon ground turmeric
8 candlenuts or cashew nuts

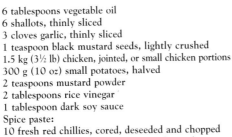

To make spice paste, put all ingredients in a blender and mix to a paste. In a large wok or sauté pan, heat oil over medium-high heat. Add shallots and garlic and fry until lightly browned. Stir in spice paste and cook for about 5 minutes, stirring. Add mustard seeds, stir once or twice then add chicken. Cook, stirring frequently, until chicken pieces turn white.

Add potatoes and 550 ml (20 fl oz/2½ cups) water. Bring to a boil, cover then simmer for 15 minutes. Stir together mustard, vinegar and soy sauce. Stir into pan, re-cover and cook for another 15-20 minutes until chicken is tender, stirring occasionally.

Serves 4-6.

AROMATIC CHICKEN

2 teaspoons tamarind paste (see page 8-9)
salt
1.5 kg (3½ lb) chicken, cut into 10 pieces, or chicken portions, chopped
12 fresh green chillies, cored, deseeded and chopped
2 small onions, chopped
5 cloves garlic, smashed
1 ripe tomato, chopped
5 tablespoons vegetable oil
4 kaffir lime leaves
1 stalk lemon grass, crushed

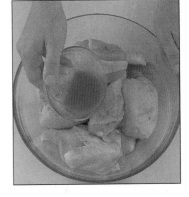

Blend tamarind with 1 teaspoon salt and 2 tablespoons hot water. Pour mixture over chicken and rub in. Leave for 1 hour.

Put chillies, onions, garlic and tomato in a blender. Mix to a paste. In a wok or large heavy sauté pan, heat oil. Add chicken and marinade. Turn to brown on both sides then remove with a slotted spoon.

Add spice paste, lime leaves and lemon grass to pan. Cook, stirring, for 6-7 minutes until paste is browned. Return chicken to pan, add 300 ml (10 fl oz/1¼ cups) water and bring to a simmer. Cover and simmer gently for 30 minutes until chicken juices run clear, turning chicken occasionally.

Serves 4.

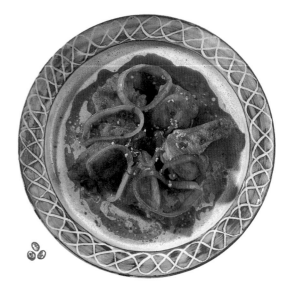

CRISPY-SKIN CHICKEN

1.5 kg (3 lb) chicken
salt
1 tablespoon golden syrup (corn syrup)
4 tablespoons plus 1 teaspoon sea salt
3½ teaspoons Chinese five-spice powder
2 tablespoons rice vinegar
925 ml (30 fl oz/3¾ cups) vegetable oil

Bring a large saucepan of salted water to the boil. Lower in chicken, return to the boil, then remove pan from heat, cover tightly and leave the chicken in the water for 30 minutes.

Drain chicken, dry with absorbent kitchen paper and leave in a cold dry place for at least 12 hours. In a small bowl, mix together golden syrup (corn syrup), 1 teaspoon salt, ½ teaspoon five-spice powder and rice vinegar. Brush over chicken and leave in the refrigerator for 20 minutes. Repeat until all the coating is used. Refrigerate the chicken for at least 4 hours to allow the coating to dry thoroughly on the skin.

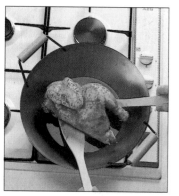

Split chicken in half, through the breast. In a wok, heat oil, add chicken halves and deep-fry for 5 minutes until golden brown. Lift chicken from oil and drain on absorbent kitchen paper. Cut into bite-size pieces. In a small saucepan over a low heat, stir together remaining sea salt and remaining five-spice powder for 2 minutes. Sprinkle over chicken.

Serves 4.

NONYA CHICKEN

2 tablespoons vegetable oil
800 g (1¾ lb) chicken portions, cut into large bite-size pieces
2 fresh red chillies, sliced into rings
1 tablespoon dark soy sauce
1 tablespoon light soy sauce
1½ teaspoons light brown sugar
1 onion, sliced into 5 mm (¼ in) rings
sesame oil for sprinkling
toasted sesame seeds, to garnish

In a wok or large frying pan (skillet) over medium-high heat, heat oil. Add chicken and fry until evenly browned.

Using a slotted spoon transfer to paper towels to drain. Add chillies to pan and stir-fry for 30 seconds. Return chicken to pan. Add soy sauces, sugar and 4 tablespoons water. Bring to a simmer. Stir, cover pan then cook gently for 10 minutes, stirring occasionally.

Stir in onion, re-cover pan and continue to cook gently, stirring occasionally, for 5 minutes or until chicken juices run clear when pierced with a sharp knife and onion is soft. Sprinkle in a few drops of sesame oil. Serve scattered with toasted sesame seeds to garnish.

Serves 3-4.

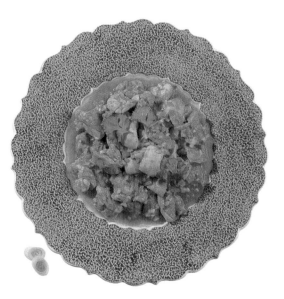

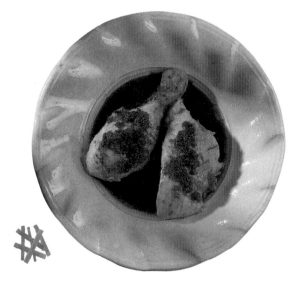

SPICED CHICKEN

8 chicken thighs, boned (see page 22) and chopped
3 tablespoons vegetable oil
1 clove garlic, finely chopped
2 tablespoons Thai fish sauce
6 shallots, finely chopped
fresh coriander (cilantro) leaves, to garnish
Marinade:
2 small fresh red chillies, cored, seeded and chopped
1 stalk lemon grass, chopped
1 clove garlic, crushed
4 cm (1½ in) piece fresh root ginger, chopped
1 tablespoon ground turmeric
225 g (8 oz) canned tomatoes
1 light brown sugar
salt

To make marinade, put all ingredients in a blender and mix together well. Put chicken in a non-reactive bowl. Pour marinade over chicken. Stir together, cover and refrigerate overnight. Return bowl of chicken to room temperature for 1 hour. In a wok or heavy sauté pan over high heat, heat oil. Add garlic and fry for 30 seconds. Add chicken and marinade. Stir and toss together then stir in fish sauce and 4 tablespoons hot water. Cover, lower heat and simmer for 5 minutes.

Add shallots and continue to cook, uncovered, stirring occasionally, for about 10 minutes until chicken juices run clear. Serve garnished with coriander (cilantro).

Serves 4.

GINGER & SOY ROAST CHICKEN

4 cm (1½ in) piece of fresh root ginger, coarsely chopped
1 onion, coarsely chopped
3 cloves garlic, coarsely chopped
1.5 kg (3½ lb) chicken
5 tablespoons vegetable oil
3 tablespoons dark soy sauce
3 tablespoons rice vinegar
2½ tablespoons light brown sugar

Put ginger, onion and garlic in a blender. Mix to a paste, adding just enough water so the blender blades work.

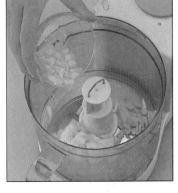

Put chicken in a roasting tin (pan). Rub inside and outside of chicken with half of ginger mixture. Cover and leave for 1 hour. Put remaining ginger paste in a bowl and stir in oil, soy sauce, rice vinegar, sugar and 6 tablespoons water.

Preheat oven to 180C/350F/Gas 4. Prop up tail end of chicken. Pour as much soy sauce mixture as possible into cavity of chicken. Roast chicken for 25 minutes, basting occasionally with remaining soy mixture. Pour remaining soy mixture around chicken and cook for a further 50 minutes, basting occasionally, until chicken juices run clear. Stir a little water into tin (pan) if sauce begins to dry out too much.

Serves 4.

STEAMED CHICKEN WITH MUSHROOMS

2 teaspoons rice wine or dry sherry
2 tablespoons light soy sauce
½ teaspoon sea salt
1 teaspoon sugar
2 tablespoons Singaporean Chicken Stock, see page 11
400 g (14 oz) can straw mushrooms, drained, liquid reserved
450 g (1 lb) boned chicken breasts, cubed
2 slices fresh root ginger, chopped
3 spring onions (scallions), coarsely chopped

In a bowl, mix together rice wine or dry sherry, soy sauce, salt, sugar, stock and reserved mushroom liquid.

Place chicken in a heatproof casserole with mushrooms, pour over contents of bowl then sprinkle with ginger and spring onions (scallions); cover casserole.

Place in a steamer, cover and cook for 10 minutes until chicken is firm and tender. Remove dish from steamer and pour off cooking liquid into a wok. Bring to the boil, simmer for 2-3 minutes, then pour over the chicken.

Serves 6.

CHICKEN WITH LEMON GRASS

450 g (1 lb) boned and skinned chicken fillet, cut into bite-size slices or cubes
salt and freshly ground black pepper
1 teaspoon finely chopped garlic
2 tablespoons finely chopped lemon grass
1 tablespoon sugar
1 teaspoon chilli sauce
3 tablespoons Thai fish sauce
2-3 tablespoons vegetable oil
1 small onion, sliced
1-2 small red chillies, deseeded and chopped

Mix chicken with salt, pepper, garlic, lemon grass, sugar, chilli sauce and 1 tablespoon fish sauce and marinate for 30 minutes.

Heat oil in a wok or frying-pan (skillet) and stir-fry onion slices for about 1 minute until opaque. Add chicken pieces, stir to separate them, then add the remaining fish sauce and cook for 2-3 minutes until the colour of chicken changes.

Add 55 ml (2 fl oz/¼ cup) water to marinade bowl to rinse out, then add to the chicken. Bring to the boil and cook for 1 minute. Garnish with the chopped chillies and serve with rice noodles.

Serves 4.

Variations: Firm white fish, pork or cubes of tofu can be cooked by the same method. Chicken stock can be used to rinse out the marinade bowl instead of water.

CHICKEN IN COCONUT MILK

CHICKEN & COCONUT CURRY

8 black peppercorns, cracked
6 coriander roots, finely chopped
4.5 cm (1¾ in) piece galangal, thinly sliced
2 fresh green chillies, deseeded and thinly sliced
550 ml (20 fl oz/2½ cups) coconut milk
grated rind 1 kaffir lime
4 kaffir lime leaves, shredded
1.35 kg (3 lb) chicken, cut into 8 pieces
1 tablespoon Thai fish sauce
3 tablespoons lime juice
3 tablespoons chopped fresh coriander (cilantro)

Using a pestle and mortar or small blender, pound or mix together peppercorns, coriander roots and galangal.

In a wok, briefly heat peppercorn mixture, stirring, then stir in chillies, coconut milk, lime peel and leaves. Heat to just simmering point and add chicken portions. Adjust heat so liquid is barely moving, then cook gently for about 40-45 minutes until chicken is very tender and liquid reduced.

Stir in fish sauce and lime juice. Scatter coriander (cilantro) leaves over chicken and serve.

Serves 6-8.

1 kg (2¼ lb) chicken, cut into 10-12 pieces
salt and freshly ground black pepper
1 teaspoon sugar
1 tablespoon curry powder
3-4 tablespoons vegetable oil
3 red or white potatoes, cut into cubes
1 teaspoon chopped garlic
1 tablespoon chopped lemon grass
1 onion, cut into small pieces
250 ml (9 fl oz/1 cup) Hot Sauce, page 119
450 ml (16 fl oz/2 cups) stock or water
450 ml (16 fl oz/2 cups) coconut milk
3 fresh bay leaves and 1 carrot, sliced
2 tablespoons Thai fish sauce
fresh coriander (cilantro) sprigs, to garnish

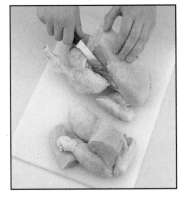

In a dish, marinate the chicken pieces with salt, pepper, sugar, and curry powder for at least 1 hour. Heat oil in a large pan and fry the potatoes for 3-4 minutes until brown - it is not necessary to completely cook the potatoes at this stage. Remove potatoes from pan and set aside.

In the same oil, stir-fry garlic, lemon grass and onion for about 30 seconds. Add the chicken pieces and stir-fry for 2-3 minutes, then add the hot sauce, stock or water, coconut milk and bay leaves. Bring to the boil, and add the par-cooked potatoes, carrot slices and fish sauce. Blend well, then cover and simmer for 15-20 minutes, stirring now and then to make sure nothing is stuck on the bottom of the pan. Garnish with coriander (cilantro) sprigs and serve.

Serves 4-6.

GRILLED CHICKEN DRUMSTICKS

CORIANDER TURKEY RICE

1-2 cloves garlic, chopped
1-2 sticks lemon grass, chopped
2 shallots, chopped
1-2 small red or green chillies, chopped
1 tablespoon chopped fresh coriander (cilantro)
55 ml (2 fl oz/¼ cup) Thai fish sauce
6-8 chicken drumsticks, skinned
TO SERVE:
lettuce leaves
Spicy Fish Sauce, page 121

Using a pestle and mortar, pound garlic, lemon grass, shallots, chillies and coriander (cilantro) to a paste.

1 tablespoon sunflower oil
2 shallots, chopped
2 cloves garlic, finely chopped
25 g (1 oz) Parma ham, trimmed and cut into strips
300 g (10 oz/1¼ cups) long-grain white rice, rinsed
1 teaspoon ground coriander
salt and freshly ground black pepper
850 ml (30 fl oz/3¾ cups) Singaporean Chicken Stock, page 11
115 g (4 oz) asparagus, cut into 2.5 cm (1 in) pieces, blanched
225 g (8 oz/2 cups) frozen peas
225 g (8 oz) cooked turkey, skinned and diced
4 tablespoons chopped fresh coriander (cilantro)

In a mixing bowl, thoroughly blend pounded mixture with the fish sauce to a smooth paste. Add drumsticks and coat well with the paste, then cover the bowl and leave to marinate for 2-3 hours, turning drumsticks every 30 minutes or so.

Heat oil in a non-stick or well seasoned wok and stir-fry shallots, garlic, ham, rice and ground coriander for 2 minutes. Season.

Prepare barbecue or preheat grill (broiler). Cook the drumsticks over barbecue or under the grill (broiler) for 10-15 minutes, turning frequently and basting with the marinade remaining in the bowl for the first 5 minutes only. Serve hot on a bed of lettuce leaves with the spicy fish sauce as a dip.

Serves 4-6.

Pour in stock and bring to the boil. Reduce heat and simmer for 20 minutes. Gently stir in asparagus, frozen peas, turkey and coriander (cilantro) and cook gently for 5 minutes until heated through, stirring to prevent sticking. Serve immediately.

Serves 4.

CHICKEN HOT POT

450 g (1 lb) chicken thigh meat, boned and cut into
small bite-sized pieces
salt and freshly ground black pepper
2 teaspoons sugar
1 tablespoon each lime juice and Thai fish sauce
1 tablespoon vegetable oil
2 cloves garlic, sliced
2 shallots, chopped
1 tablespoon dried small red chillies
2 tablespoons crushed yellow bean sauce
about 450 ml (16 fl oz/2 cups) Singaporean Chicken
Stock, page 12
2 spring onions (scallions), cut into short sections
coriander sprigs, to garnish

Marinate the chicken with salt, pepper,
sugar, lime juice and fish sauce for 1-2 hours.

Heat the oil in a clay pot or flameproof casserole and stir-fry garlic, shallots and chillies
for about 1 minute, then add yellow bean
sauce and stir until smooth.

Add the chicken pieces and stir-fry for 1-2
minutes. Add chicken stock, blend well and
bring to the boil, then reduce heat, cover and
simmer gently for 15-20 minutes. Uncover
and stir in spring onions (scallions). Garnish
with coriander (cilantro) sprigs and serve
straight from the pot. Serve with rice.

Serves 4.

Note: The longer the chicken is marinated,
the better the flavour, so try and leave it for
2 hours.

SWEET & SOUR TURKEY

450 g (1 lb) skinless, boneless turkey
1 tablespoon sunflower oil
2 shallots, chopped
2 sticks celery, sliced
2 tablespoons light soy sauce
1 red pepper (capsicum), sliced
1 yellow pepper (capsicum), sliced
1 green pepper (capsicum), sliced
115 g (4 oz) canned bamboo shoots, drained
3 tablespoons plum sauce
2 tablespoons white rice vinegar
1 teaspoon sesame oil
2 tablespoons sesame seeds

Trim away any excess fat from turkey. Cut
into 2.5 cm (1 in) cubes. Heat oil in a non-
stick or well seasoned wok and stir-fry turkey,
shallots and celery for 2-3 minutes until
lightly coloured.

Add soy sauce and peppers (capsicum) and
stir-fry for 2 minutes. Stir in bamboo shoots,
plum sauce and vinegar and simmer gently
for 2 minutes. Stir in sesame oil, sprinkle
with sesame seeds and serve.

Serves 4.

TURKEY & BAMBOO CURRY

GRILLED QUAIL

3 tablespoons unsweetened desiccated coconut,
  soaked in 150 ml (5 fl oz/⅔ cup) boiling water for
  30 minutes
450 g (1 lb) skinless, boneless turkey
1 tablespoon sunflower oil
1 clove garlic, finely chopped
1 cm (½ in) piece fresh root ginger, finely chopped
4 spring onions (scallions), chopped
175 g (6 oz) baby sweetcorn
2 tablespoons dark soy sauce
1 cinnamon stick, broken
1 teaspoon ground coriander
150 ml (5 fl oz/⅔ cup) Singaporean Chicken Stock,
  page 11
115 g (4 oz) canned bamboo shoots, drained

4 cleaned quail, each split down the backbone and
  pressed flat
salt and freshly ground black pepper
1 teaspoon finely chopped garlic
1 tablespoon finely chopped lemon grass
1 teaspoon sugar
1 tablespoon Thai fish sauce
1 tablespoon lime juice or vinegar
1-2 tablespoons vegetable oil
lettuce leaves
coriander sprigs, to garnish
Spicy Fish Sauce, page 121, to serve

Rub the 4 quail all over with plenty of salt
and pepper.

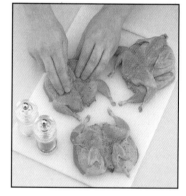

Pour coconut mixture through a fine sieve
(strainer) placed over a bowl, pressing the
coconut with the back of a spoon to extract
all the liquid. Reserve liquid and discard
coconut. Trim away any excess fat from
turkey. Cut into 1 cm (½ in) strips. Heat oil
in a non-stick or well seasoned wok and stir-
fry turkey, garlic, ginger, spring onions (scallions) and baby sweetcorn for 2 minutes
until turkey is lightly coloured.

In a mixing bowl, blend garlic, lemon grass,
sugar, fish sauce and lime juice or vinegar.
Add quail, turning to coat in the mixture,
then leave to marinate for 2-3 hours, turning
over now and then.

Stir in soy sauce, cinnamon stick, ground
coriander, coconut water and stock. Bring to
the boil and simmer gently for 20 minutes.
Stir in bamboo shoots and simmer gently for
5 minutes. Discard cinnamon sticks and
serve with rice and salad.

Serves 4.

Prepare a barbecue or preheat grill. Brush
quail with oil and cook over barbecue or
under grill for 6-8 minutes each side, basting
with remaining marinade during first 5
minutes of cooking. Serve quail on a bed of
lettuce leaves, garnished with coriander
sprigs, accompanied by spicy fish sauce as a
dip.

Serves 4.

SPICED TURKEY STIR-FRY

450 g (1 lb) lean, boneless turkey
1 egg white, lightly beaten
large pinch of salt
1 teaspoon cornflour (cornstarch)
1 tablespoon sunflower oil
½ teaspoon Szechuan peppercorns, toasted and
  crushed
225 g (8 oz) Szechuan preserved vegetables,
  shredded
225 g (8 oz) mange tout (snow peas)
115 g (4 oz) canned water chestnuts, rinsed and
  sliced

Skin and trim turkey. Cut into thin strips
about 5 mm (¼ in) thick.

Place turkey strips in a bowl and mix with
egg white, salt and cornflour (cornstarch).
Cover and chill for 30 minutes.

Heat the oil in a non-stick or well seasoned
wok and stir-fry turkey with crushed peppercorns for 2 minutes until turkey is just
coloured. Add remaining ingredients and
stir-fry for 3 minutes until just cooked
through. Serve immediately.

Serves 4.

DUCK CURRY

5 tablespoons coconut cream, see page 8-9
5 tablespoons green curry paste
about 1.35 kg (3 lb) duck, skinned if desired, well-
  trimmed of excess fat, divided into 8 portions
550 ml (20 fl oz/2½ cups) coconut milk
1 tablespoon Thai fish sauce
8 kaffir lime leaves, shredded
2 fresh green chillies, deseeded and thinly sliced
12 fresh Thai holy basil leaves
leaves from 5 coriander sprigs
fresh coriander (cilantro) sprigs, to garnish

Heat coconut cream in a wok over a medium
heat, stirring, until it thickens and oil begins
to separate and bubble.

Stir in curry paste and cook for about 5
minutes until mixture darkens. Stir in duck
pieces to coat with curry mixture. Lower
heat, cover and cook for 15 minutes, stirring
occasionally. If necessary, using a bulb baster,
remove excess fat from the surface, or carefully spoon it off. Stir in coconut milk, fish
sauce and lime leaves. Heat to just simmering point, then cook gently without boiling,
turning duck over occasionally, for 30-40
minutes until meat is very tender. Remove
surplus fat from surface, then stir in chillies.

Cook for a further 5 minutes. Stir in basil
and coriander (cilantro) leaves and cook for
a further 2 minutes. Garnish with coriander
(cilantro) sprigs.

Serves 4.

DUCK WITH KIWI FRUIT

2 × 225 g (8 oz) boneless duck breasts
1 cm (½ in) piece fresh root ginger, finely chopped
1 clove garlic, finely chopped
2 tablespoons dry sherry
2 kiwi fruit
1 teaspoon sesame oil
Sauce:
4 tablespoons dry sherry
2 tablespoons light soy sauce
4 teaspoons clear honey

Skin and trim duck breasts. With a sharp knife, score flesh in diagonal lines. Beat with a meat tenderizer until 1 cm (½ in) thick.

Place duck breasts in a shallow dish and add ginger, garlic and sherry. Cover and chill for 1 hour. Peel and thinly slice kiwi fruit and halve widthways. Cover and chill until required. Preheat grill (broiler). Drain duck breasts and place on grill rack. Brush with sesame oil and cook for 8 minutes. Turn and brush again with oil. Cook for 8-10 minutes until tender and cooked through.

Meanwhile, put the sauce ingredients in a saucepan, bring to the boil and simmer for 5 until syrupy. Drain duck breasts on kitchen paper and slice thinly. Arrange duck slices and kiwi fruit on serving plates. Pour over sauce.

Serves 4.

SOY-ROASTED DUCK

2.25 kg (5 lb) duck, giblets removed
4 tablespoons dark soy sauce
2 tablespoons brown sugar
2 cloves garlic, finely chopped
Dip:
1 tablespoon sunflower oil
4 spring onions (scallions), finely chopped
1 clove garlic, finely chopped
3 tablespoons dark soy sauce
2 teaspoons brown sugar
2 tablespoons dry sherry

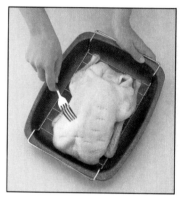

Preheat oven to 190C (375F/Gas 5). Wash duckling and pat dry. Place on a wire rack in a roasting tin (pan). Prick all over with a fork.

Sprinkle over soy sauce, brown sugar and garlic. Bake for 2¼ hours until juices run clear and skin is well browned. Make the dip. Heat the oil in a non-stick or well seasoned wok and stir-fry spring onions (scallions) and garlic for 1 minute. Drain on kitchen paper and mix with remaining ingredients.

To serve, remove all skin and fat from duckling and shred flesh away from bone. Serve with the dip, soft pancakes and shredded spring onions (scallions) and cucumber.

Serves 4.

Note: Soft pancakes can be bought ready-made from Chinese supermarkets.

AROMATIC DUCK

2 half or 4 quarter portions of duck (2 breasts and 2 legs)
salt and freshly ground black pepper
1 tablespoon five-spice powder
4-5 small pieces fresh root ginger
3-4 spring onions (scallions), cut into short sections
3-4 tablespoons Chinese rice wine or dry sherry
12 sheets dried rice paper, halved if large
fresh mint, basil and coriander (cilantro) leaves
Spicy Fish Sauce, page 121 to serve

Rub the salt, pepper and five-spice powder all over the duck portions.

In a shallow dish, mix ginger, spring onions (scallions) and rice wine or sherry, add duck portions and leave to marinate for at least 3-4 hours, turning the duck pieces now and then. Steam the duck portions with marinade in a hot steamer for 2-3 hours. Remove the duck portions from the liquid and leave to cool (the duck can be cooked up to this stage in advance, if wished).

Preheat oven to 230C (450F/Gas 8) and bake the duck pieces, skin-side up, for 10-15 minutes, then pull the meat off the bone. Meanwhile, soften dried rice paper in warm water. Place about 2 tablespoons of meat in each half sheet of rice paper, add a few mint, basil and coriander leaves, roll into a neat bundle, then dip the roll in the spicy fish sauce before eating it.

Serves 4-6.

SPICED ROAST DUCK

1 teaspoon finely chopped garlic
2-3 shallots, finely chopped
2 teaspoons Chinese five-spice powder
2 tablespoons sugar
55 ml (2 fl oz/¼ cup) red rice vinegar
1 tablespoon Chinese fish sauce
1 tablespoon soy sauce
4 quarter portions duck (2 breasts and 2 legs)
250 ml (9 fl oz/1 cup) coconut milk
salt and freshly ground black pepper
watercress, to serve
fresh coriander (cilantro) sprigs, to garnish

In a bowl, mix garlic, shallots, five-spice powder, sugar, vinegar, fish and soy sauce.

Add duck pieces and leave to marinate for at least 2-3 hours, or overnight in the refrigerator, turning occasionally. Preheat oven to 220C (425F/Gas 7). Remove duck portions from marinade and place, skin-side up, on a rack in a baking tin (pan) and cook in the oven for 45 minutes, without turning or basting.

Remove duck and keep warm. Heat the marinade with the drippings in the baking tin (pan), add the coconut milk, bring to boil and simmer for 5 minutes. Season with salt and pepper, then pour sauce into a serving bowl. Serve duck portions on a bed of watercress, garnished with coriander (cilantro) sprigs.

Serves 4-6

Note: The duck portions can be chopped through the bone into bite-size pieces for serving, if wished.

MEAT DISHES

SINGAPORE STEAMBOAT

175 g (6 oz) fillet of beef, well chilled
175 g (6 oz) pork fillet (tenderloin), well chilled
175 g (6 oz) lamb fillet, well chilled
175 g (6 oz) boneless, skinless chicken breast, well chilled
350 g (12 oz) thin rice noodles
115 g (4 oz) each mange-tout (snow peas), French beans, baby sweetcorn, oyster mushrooms, shiitake mushrooms, asparagus spears, cut into bite-size pieces

Thinly slice beef, pork, lamb and chicken. Cover with cling film and set aside. Cook noodles according to instructions on package. Drain, refresh under running water. Drain again, cover and set aside.

PRAWN (SHRIMP) BALLS
350 g (12 oz) raw, peeled prawns (shrimp)
1½-2½ teaspoons cornflour (cornstarch)
2 small spring onions (scallions), finely chopped
1 small egg white, lightly beaten

Put prawns (shrimp) and 1½ teaspoons cornflour (cornstarch) into blender and mix until smooth. Mix in spring onion (scallion). Stir in egg white and more cornflour (cornstarch) if necessary to bind mixture, which should be firm enough to handle. With wet hands, roll mixture into walnut-size balls. Refrigerate until required.

CHILLI VINEGAR
3 tablespoons rice vinegar
1½ tablespoons water
2 teaspoons sugar
½-1 fresh red chilli, cored, deseeded and finely sliced

In a bowl, mix all the ingredients together.

Dipping sauce
2 tablespoons tomato purée (paste)
2 tablespoons water
1 teaspoon soy sauce
1 teaspoon toasted sesame oil
1 fresh red chilli, cored, deseeded and finely chopped

In a bowl, mix all the ingredients together.

Coconut sauce
2 teaspoons groundnut oil
1 small onion, finely chopped
5 cm (2 in) lemon grass stalk, bruised and thinly sliced
¼ teaspoon crushed coriander seeds
85 g (3 oz) piece of coconut cream
about 3 tablespoons stock

In a frying pan (skillet) or saucepan, heat oil. Add onion, lemon grass and coriander seeds and fry until the onion has softened. Stir in coconut cream until melted. Add enough stock to make a dipping sauce.

Stock
1 litre (35 fl oz/scant 4¼ cups) Singaporean Chicken or Vegetable Stock, see pages 11 and 12
1½ tablespoons chopped fresh coriander (cilantro)
5 cm (2 in) thick end of lemon grass stalk, thinly sliced
2 spring onions (scallions), thinly sliced

In a saucepan, bring stock ingredients to the boil, then pour into a warm fondue pot or heavy flameproof casserole set over a burner. To serve, dip the meat, prawn (shrimp) balls and vegetables into the stock to cook, then transfer them to plates to eat with the sauces and chilli vinegar.

When all the meat, fish and vegetables have been eaten, either warm the noodles in the hotpot, or dunk them in a bowl or saucepan of boiling water, then drain and divide them among bowls. Ladle remaining stock, which will have become concentrated, into the bowls.

Serves 6.

To serve: Use fondue forks, chopsticks, Chinese wire mesh baskets or long wooden skewers.

LAMB CHOPS WITH CHILLI SAUCE

1 tablespoon hoisin sauce
1 tablespoon dark soy sauce
2 cloves garlic, finely chopped
1 teaspoon sea salt
¼ teaspoon ground white pepper
4 lamb chops, 175-225 g (6-8 oz) each
2 tablespoons peanut oil
2 onions, sliced
55 ml (2 fl oz/¼ cup) Singaporean Vegetable Stock,
  see page 12

Sauce:
1 fresh hot red chilli, deseeded and sliced
1 hot fresh green chilli, deseeded and sliced
½ teaspoon sea salt
1 tablespoon lemon juice

1 teaspoon brown sugar
2 tablespoons peanut oil

In a bowl, mix together hoisin sauce, soy sauce, garlic, salt and pepper. Coat chops with mixture and leave for 1 hour.

In a wok, heat oil until smoking, add onions and fry for 2 minutes until transparent. Reduce heat, add chops and cook for about 5 minutes each side. Add stock, cover and gently cook for 5 minutes. In a bowl, mix together all sauce ingredients, pour into a small saucepan and heat gently. Transfer chops to a warmed serving plate and pour over sauce.

Serves 4.

STIR-FRIED SESAME LAMB

350 g (12 oz) lean lamb fillet
1 tablespoon sunflower oil
115 g (4 oz) shallots, sliced
1 red pepper (capsicum), sliced
1 green pepper (capsicum), sliced
1 clove garlic, finely chopped
1 tablespoon light soy sauce
1 teaspoon white rice vinegar
1 teaspoon caster sugar
freshly ground black pepper
2 tablespoons sesame seeds

Trim any fat and silver skin from the lamb fillet. Cut into 5 mm (¼ in) cubes.

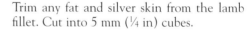

Heat oil in a non-stick or well seasoned wok and stir-fry the lamb for 1-2 minutes until browned. Remove with a slotted spoon and set aside. Stir-fry shallots, peppers (capsicum) and garlic for 2 minutes until just soft.

Return lamb to wok with all the remaining ingredients except the sesame seeds. Stir-fry for 2 minutes. Sprinkle with sesame seeds and serve with rice and vegetables.

Serves 4.

LAMB WITH SPINACH

3 tablespoons soy sauce
¼ teaspoon Chinese five-spice powder
2.5 cm (1 in) piece fresh root ginger, cut into
   julienne strips
2 cloves garlic, finely chopped
700 g (1½ lb) lamb fillet, cut crosswise into thin strips
1 tablespoon sesame oil
1 fresh red chilli, seeded and thinly sliced
8 spring onions (scallions), cut into 5 cm (2 in) pieces
1 mango, peeled and cut into 1 cm (½ in) thick
   pieces
175 g (6 oz) fresh baby spinach leaves, washed and
   dried
3 tablespoons dry sherry or rice wine
1 teaspoon cornflour (cornstarch) dissolved in 1
   tablespoon water

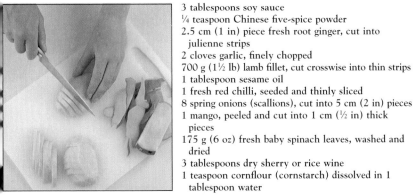

In a shallow baking dish, combine soy sauce, five-spice powder, ginger and garlic. Add lamb strips and toss to coat well. Leave to marinate for 1 hour, covered, stirring occasionally. Heat the wok until very hot. Add sesame oil and swirl to coat. With a slotted spoon and working in 2 batches, add lamb to wok, draining off and reserving as much marinade as possible. Stir-fry lamb for 2-3 minutes until browned on all sides. Remove to a bowl. Add chilli to oil remaining in wok and stir-fry for 1 minute.

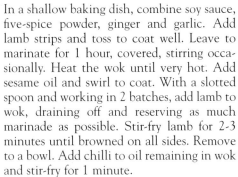

Add spring onions (scallions) and mango and stir-fry for 1 minute. Stir in spinach leaves, reserved lamb, dry sherry or rice wine and reserved marinade. Stir cornflour (cornstarch) mixture and stir into wok. Stir-fry for 1 minute, tossing all ingredients until spinach wilts and lamb is lightly glazed with sauce.

Serves 4.

LAMB WITH STAR ANISE

4 × 150 g (5 oz) lean lamb loin chops
2 teaspoons sunflower oil
1 clove garlic, thinly sliced
4 star anise
1 tablespoon light soy sauce
4 tablespoons dry sherry
1 teaspoon caster sugar
salt and ground white pepper
1 teaspoon cornflour (cornstarch) mixed with 2
   teaspoons water
2 spring onions (scallions), shredded, to garnish

Trim any rind, fat and bone from the lamb. Using string, tie the lamb into round steaks.

Heat oil in a non-stick or well seasoned wok, add the garlic and lamb and fry for 2 minutes on each side until browned. Drain on kitchen paper and wipe out wok. Return lamb and garlic to wok. Add star anise, soy sauce, sherry, sugar and salt and pepper.

Bring to the boil, reduce heat and simmer for 4 minutes, turning lamb halfway through. Add cornflour (cornstarch) mixture and cook, stirring, until thickened. Simmer for 2 minutes. Discard star anise and remove string from lamb before serving. Garnish with spring onions and serve with rice and vegetables.

Serves 4.

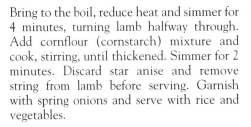

LAMB WITH SPICY HOT SAUCE

300 g (10 oz) lamb steak, thinly sliced
salt and freshly ground black pepper
1 teaspoon finely chopped garlic
1 teaspoon chopped fresh root ginger
1 tablespoon Thai fish sauce
3 tablespoons vegetable oil
225 g (8 oz) spinach or any green vegetable
1 tablespoon oyster sauce
2-3 tablespoons Hot Sauce, page 119
about 2-3 tablespoons stock or water
½ teaspoon sesame oil
fresh mint and/or coriander (cilantro) sprigs, to
 garnish

Marinate the lamb slices with salt, pepper, garlic, ginger, and fish sauce for 2-3 hours.

Heat about half of the oil in a wok or pan and stir-fry the spinach or green vegetable for about 2 minutes. Blend in the oyster sauce, then place on a warmed serving dish.

Wipe clean the wok or pan and add the remaining oil. When hot, add the lamb slices and hot sauce and stir-fry for 2 minutes. Rinse out remaining marinade with stock or water and add to the lamb. Bring to the boil and braise for 2-3 minutes, stirring all the time. Add the sesame oil, then spoon the lamb over the spinach or green vegetable. Garnish with mint and/or coriander (cilantro) sprigs and serve at once.

Serves 4.

MIXED VEGETABLES & PORK

225 g (8 oz) lean pork, finely chopped
freshly ground black pepper
2 tablespoons vegetable oil
3 cloves garlic, finely chopped
450 g (1 lb) prepared mixed vegetables, such as
 mange tout (snow peas), broccoli flowerets, red
 pepper (capsicum) and courgettes (zucchini)
1 tablespoon Thai fish sauce
½ teaspoon crushed palm sugar
3 spring onions (scallions), finely chopped

In a bowl, mix together pork and plenty of black pepper. Set aside for 30 minutes.

In a wok or frying pan (skillet), heat oil, add garlic and cook, stirring occasionally, for 2-3 minutes, then stir in pork.

Stir briefly until pork changes colour. Stir in mixed vegetables, then fish sauce, sugar and 115 ml (4 fl oz/½ cup) water. Stir for 3-4 minutes until mange tout (snow peas) are bright green and vegetables still crisp. Stir in spring onions (scallions).

Serves 4.

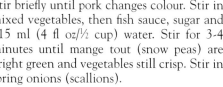

SPICY PORK & LEMON GRASS

1 clove garlic, chopped
2 shallots, chopped
3 tablespoons chopped lemon grass
1 tablespoon sugar
1 tablespoon Thai fish sauce
salt and freshly ground black pepper
350 g (12 oz) pork fillet, cut into small, thin slices
2-3 tablespoons vegetable oil
2-3 sticks celery, thinly sliced
115 g (4 oz) straw mushrooms, halved lengthwise
4 small red chillies, deseeded and shredded
2 spring onions (scallions), shredded
1 tablespoon soy sauce
about 55 ml (2 fl oz/¼ cup) stock or water
2 teaspoons cornflour (cornstarch)
coriander sprigs, to garnish

Using a pestle and mortar, pound the garlic, shallots and lemon grass to a paste. Transfer to a mixing bowl and add the sugar, fish sauce, salt and pepper. Blend well, then add the pork slices, turning to coat them with the mixture, and leave to marinate for 25-30 minutes.

Heat oil in a wok or frying-pan (skillet) and stir-fry pork slices for 2 minutes. Add the celery, straw mushrooms, chillies, spring onions (scallions) and soy sauce and stir-fry for 2-3 minutes. Use the stock to rinse out the marinade bowl and add to the pork. Bring to the boil. Mix cornflour (cornstarch) with 1 tablespoon water and add to sauce to thicken it. Garnish with coriander (cilantro) sprigs and serve at once with a mixture of rice and wild rice.

Serves 4.

YELLOW BEAN LAMB

115 g (4 oz) transparent vermicelli rice noodles
350 g (12 oz) lean boneless lamb
1 tablespoon groundnut (peanut) oil
1 clove garlic, finely chopped
2 spring onions (scallions), finely chopped
115 g (4 oz) mange tout (snow peas), sliced
2 tablespoons yellow bean sauce
freshly ground black pepper
2 tablespoons chopped fresh chives, to garnish

Bring a saucepan of water to the boil. Remove from heat and add noodles. Leave to soak for 2-3 minutes until soft, then drain well and set aside.

Trim any fat from the lamb and cut into 5 mm (½ in) strips. Heat oil in a non-stick or well seasoned wok and stir-fry lamb, garlic, spring onions (scallions) and mange tout (snow peas) for 2-3 minutes until lamb is browned.

Stir in yellow bean sauce and noodles, season with black pepper and stir-fry for 3 minutes. Garnish with chopped chives and serve with a mixed salad.

Serves 4.

RED-COOKED LAMB FILLET

450 g (1 lb) lean lamb fillet
3 tablespoons dry sherry
1 cm (½ in) piece fresh root ginger, finely chopped
2 cloves garlic, thinly sliced
1 teaspoon five-spice powder
3 tablespoons dark soy sauce
300 ml (10 fl oz/1¼ cups) Singaporean Vegetable
  Stock, page 12
2 teaspoons caster sugar
2 teaspoons cornflour (cornstarch) mixed with 4
  teaspoons water
salt and freshly ground black pepper
shredded spring onions (scallions), to garnish

Trim any excess fat and silver skin from lamb and cut into 2 cm (¾ in) cubes.

Blanch the lamb in a saucepan of boiling water for 3 minutes. Drain well. Heat a non-stick or well seasoned wok and add the lamb with the sherry, ginger, garlic, five-spice powder and soy sauce. Bring to the boil, reduce heat and simmer for 2 minutes, stirring. Pour in stock, return to the boil and simmer for 25 minutes.

Add sugar, cornflour (cornstarch) mixture and seasoning and stir until thickened. Simmer gently for 5 minutes. Garnish with shredded spring onions (scallions).

Serves 4.

STIR-FRIED PORK

1 teaspoon finely chopped garlic
2 shallots, finely chopped
½ teaspoon chopped fresh root ginger
1 teaspoon sugar
1 tablespoon fish sauce
salt and freshly ground black pepper
450 g (1 lb) pork fillet, cut into small slices or cubes
2-3 tablespoons vegetable oil
115 g (4 oz) sliced bamboo shoots, drained
2 small red chillies, deseeded and chopped
2 spring onions (scallions), chopped
2 tablespoons oyster sauce
about 55 ml (2 fl oz/¼ cup) stock or water
2 teaspoons cornflour (cornstarch)
½ teaspoon sesame oil
coriander sprigs, to garnish

In a bowl, mix garlic, shallots, ginger, sugar, fish sauce and salt and pepper. Add pork and leave to marinate for 25-30 minutes.

Heat oil in a wok or frying-pan (skillet) and stir-fry pork pieces for 2 minutes, then add bamboo shoots, chillies, spring onions (scallions) and oyster sauce and stir-fry for 4-5 minutes. Rinse out the marinade bowl with the stock or water and add to the pork mixture. Bring to the boil. Mix cornflour (cornstarch) with 1 tablespoon water and stir into sauce. Cook, stirring, until thickened. Add sesame oil and garnish with coriander sprigs.

Serves 4.

LAMB IN GARLIC SAUCE

450 g (1 lb) lamb tenderloin, very thinly sliced
3 tablespoons dark soy sauce
5 tablespoons peanut oil
1 tablespoon rice wine or dry sherry
½ teaspoon sea salt
2 cloves garlic, chopped
8 spring onions (scallions), chopped
1 tablespoon rice vinegar
½ teaspoon ground Szechuan peppercorns
2 tablespoons sesame oil

HOT SWEET PORK

350 g (12 oz) lean pork fillet
1 tablespoon light soy sauce
1 tablespoon rice wine
freshly ground black pepper
1 tablespoon cornflour (cornstarch)
1 tablespoon sunflower oil
2 fresh red chillies, seeded and chopped
1 clove garlic, finely chopped
1 red pepper (capsicum), diced
225 g (8 oz) courgettes (zucchini), diced
115 g (4 oz) canned bamboo shoots, drained
2 tablespoons red rice vinegar
2 tablespoon brown sugar
large pinch of salt
1 tablespoon sesame seeds
strips of fresh red chilli, to garnish

Lay lamb in a shallow dish. In a bowl, mix together 1 soy sauce, 2 tablespoons peanut oil, the rice wine or dry sherry, salt and Szechuan peppercorns. Pour over lamb, turn to coat then leave for 30 minutes.

Trim any fat and silver skin from the pork fillet. Cut into 1 cm (½ in) strips. Place in a bowl and mix with soy sauce, rice wine, black pepper and cornflour (cornstarch). Cover and chill for 30 minutes.

In a wok, heat remaining peanut oil until smoking, add garlic and lamb. Stir-fry for 2 minutes until lamb just changes colour; remove from wok. Pour oil from wok, leaving just 1 tablespoonful. Add spring onions (scallions) and stir-fry for 2 minutes. Add remaining soy sauce and the vinegar. Continue stir-frying for another minute then add the lamb slices and sesame oil. Stir-fry for 1 minute making sure lamb and sauce are thoroughly mixed.

Serves 4.

Heat oil in a non-stick or well seasoned wok and stir-fry pork mixture for 1-2 minutes until pork is browned. Add remaining ingredients except the sesame seeds and garnish and continue to stir-fry for a further 4-5 minutes until vegetables are just cooked through. Sprinkle with sesame seeds, garnish with chilli strips and serve with noodles.

Serves 4.

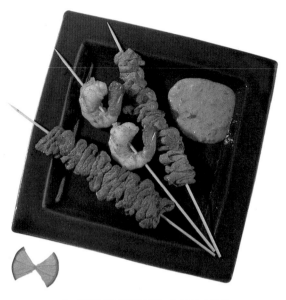

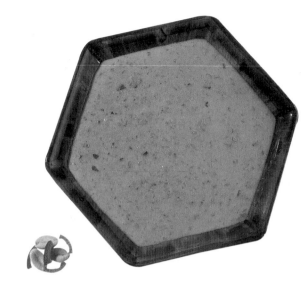

MIXED SATAY

SATAY SAUCE

350 g (12 oz) pork fillet, chilled, thinly sliced
350 g (12 oz) steak, chilled, thinly sliced
½ lime
2 teaspoons each ground coriander and ground cumin
1 teaspoon ground turmeric
1 tablespoon light brown sugar
4 tablespoons coconut milk
12 large raw prawns (jumbo shrimp), peeled, tails left on, deveined
oil for brushing
Satay Sauce (right)

Lay each pork slice between sheets of cling film and beat with a rolling pin until fairly thin. Cut slices into 2.5 cm (1 in) wide strips.

Cut steak into strips about same size as pork. Put meats into a non-reactive bowl. Squeeze lime juice over. In a small bowl, mix together coriander, cumin, turmeric, sugar and coconut milk to make a fairly dry paste. Add prawns (shrimp) to dish with meat and spoon coconut mixture over to coat thoroughly. Cover and marinate for 1 hour, or overnight in the refrigerator.

Heat barbecue or grill (broiler). Soak bamboo skewers in water or 20-30 minutes. Thread pork strips, steak strips and shrimp (prawns) on to separate skewers. Brush with oil and cook at a very high heat for 10 minutes, turning frequently. Prawns (shrimp) should have turned opaque with bright pink tails, pork should be cooked through and beef still be pink in centre. Meanwhile, heat satay sauce. Serve sauce with the skewers.

Serves 6.

85 g (3 oz) roasted peanuts
1 fresh red chilli, cored, seeded and chopped
1 clove garlic, chopped
4 tablespoons red curry paste
375 ml (13 fl oz/scant 1¾ cups) coconut milk
squeeze of lime juice
2 tablespoons light brown sugar

Put peanuts, chilli and garlic in a blender. Mix together, then add curry paste, 2 tablespoons of the coconut milk and a squeeze of lime juice. Mix to blend evenly.

Pour mixture into a saucepan. Stir in remaining coconut milk and the sugar. Bring to a boil, stirring, then boil for 2 minutes.

Lower heat and simmer for 10 minutes, stirring occasionally. Add a little water if sauce becomes too thick.

Serves 6.

SPICY PORK HOT POT

1 tablespoon vegetable oil
2 cloves garlic, chopped
2 shallots, chopped
450 g (1 lb) lean pork, cut into bite-size pieces
3 tablespoons sugar
3 tablespoons Thai fish sauce
1 teaspoon Chinese five-spice powder
about 250 ml (9 fl oz/1 cup) stock or water
salt and freshly ground black pepper
2-3 spring onions (scallions), cut into short sections,
 to garnish

Heat oil in a clay pot or flameproof casserole and stir-fry the garlic and shallots for about 1 minute until fragrant.

Add the pork pieces and stir-fry them for about 2 minutes, or until the pork turns almost white in colour.

Add sugar, fish sauce and five-spice powder, stir for 1 minutes, then add stock or water. Bring to boil, reduce heat, cover and simmer for 15-20 minutes. Adjust seasoning, garnish with spring onions (scallions) and serve with mange tout (snow peas) and peppers (capsicums).

Serves 4.

Variation: Chicken, lamb, veal or beef can all be used instead; for lamb and veal, 25 minutes for beef.

BARBECUED SPARE RIBS

2 tablespoons chopped coriander stalks
3 cloves garlic, chopped
1 teaspoon black peppercorns, cracked
1 teaspoon grated kaffir lime peel
1 tablespoon Thai green curry paste
2 teaspoons fish sauce
1½ teaspoons crushed palm sugar
175 ml (6 fl oz/¾ cup) coconut milk
900 g (2 lb) pork spare ribs
spring onion (scallion) brushes, to garnish

Using a pestle and mortar or small blender, pound or mix together coriander, garlic, peppercorns, lime peel, curry paste, fish sauce and sugar. Stir in coconut milk. Place spare ribs in a shallow dish and pour over spiced coconut mixture. Cover and leave in a cool place for 3 hours, basting occasionally.

Preheat a barbecue or medium grill (broiler). Cook ribs for about 5 minutes a side, until cooked through and brown, basting occasionally with coconut mixture. Garnish with spring onion (scallion) brushes.

Serves 4-6.

Note: The ribs can also be cooked on a rack in a roasting tin (pan) in an oven preheated to 200C (400F/Gas 6) for 45-60 minutes, basting occasionally.

SPINACH & PORK BALLS

225 g (8 oz) fresh spinach, tough stalks removed
4 spring onions (scallions), finely chopped
350 g (12 oz 1½ cups) lean minced (ground) pork
1 clove garlic, finely chopped
1 egg white
2 tablespoons cornflour (cornstarch)
salt and freshly ground black pepper
DIP:
2 tablespoons light soy sauce
1 clove garlic, finely chopped
2 tablespoons dry sherry
1 teaspoon brown sugar

Blanch spinach in boiling salted water for a few seconds until soft. Drain and rinse in cold water. Dry on kitchen paper and shred.

In a bowl, mix together the spinach, spring onions (scallions), minced (ground) pork, garlic, egg white, cornflour (cornstarch) and seasoning. Bring together to form a dough-like mixture and divide into 16 portions. Roll each portion into a ball, flouring the hands with extra cornflour (cornstarch) to prevent sticking.

Bring a wok or large saucepan of water to the boil. Arrange pork balls on a layer of baking parchment in a steamer, put over the water, cover and steam for 8-10 minutes until cooked through. Mix together the dip ingredients. Serve the pork balls with the dip and steamed vegetables.

Serves 4.

PORK WITH VEGETABLES

225 g (8 oz) pork fillet, thinly shredded
salt and freshly ground black pepper
3 tablespoons vegetable oil
2 shallots, finely chopped
1 teaspoon chopped fresh root ginger
225 g (8 oz) bean sprouts
1 small red pepper (capsicum), thinly sliced
2-3 spring onions (scallions), shredded
2 tablespoons soy sauce
fresh coriander (cilantro) sprigs, to garnish

In a bowl, season the pork with salt and pepper and leave for 10-15 minutes.

Heat oil in a wok or frying pan (skillet) and stir-fry the shallots and ginger for about 1 minute. Add the pork and stir-fry for 2-3 minutes, until the shreds are separated and the pork turns almost white in colour.

Add bean sprouts, red pepper (capsicum), spring onions (scallions) and soy sauce and stir-fry for a further 2-3 minutes. Garnish with coriander (cilantro) sprigs and serve at once.

Serves 4.

PORK WITH TAMARIND

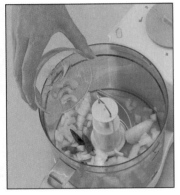

4 dried red chillies, cored and deseeded
1 large onion, chopped
4 candlenuts or cashew nuts
2 tablespoons vegetable oil
700 g (1½ lb) pork shoulder, cut into large bite-size pieces
2 tablespoons tamarind paste (see page 8-9)
2 tablespoons dark soy sauce
1 tablespoon yellow bean sauce
1 tablespoon light brown sugar
sliced fresh chillies, to garnish (optional)

Put chillies in a blender. Add 4 tablespoons hot water and leave until slightly softened. Add onion and nuts; mix to a smooth paste.

In a sauté pan, preferably non-stick, heat oil over medium-high heat. Add meat in batches and fry until an even light brown. Using a slotted spoon transfer to paper towels to drain.

Add chilli paste to pan and fry for about 5 minutes. Stir in pork, tamarind paste, soy sauce, yellow bean sauce, sugar and 350 ml (12 fl oz/1½ cups) water. Bring to a simmer, cover pan then cook gently for 30-40 minutes, stirring occasionally, until pork is very tender. Serve garnished with sliced fresh chillies, if liked.

Serves 4.

PORK WITH SPRING ONIONS

550 ml (20 fl oz/2½ cups) coconut milk
450 g (1 lb) lean pork, cut into 2.5 cm (1 in) cubes
1 tablespoon Thai fish sauce
½ teaspoon crushed palm sugar
100 g (3½ oz/1 cup) skinned peanuts
3 fresh red chillies, deseeded and chopped
3 cm (1¼ in) piece galangal, chopped
4 cloves garlic
1 stalk lemon grass, chopped
4 tablespoons coconut cream, see page 8-9
8 spring onions (scallions), chopped
1 kg (2 lb) young spinach leaves
warmed coconut cream, see page 8-9, and dry-roasted peanuts, to serve

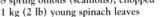

In a wok, heat coconut milk just to simmering point, adjust heat so liquid barely moves. Add pork and cook for about 25 minutes until very tender. Meanwhile, using a small blender or food processor, mix fish sauce, sugar, peanuts, chillies, galangal, garlic and lemon grass to a paste. In another wok, or a frying pan (skillet), heat coconut cream until oil separates. Add spring onions (scallions) and peanut paste and cook, stirring frequently, for 2-3 minutes.

Stir in milk from pork and boil until lightly thickened. Pour over pork, stir and cook for 5 minutes more. Rinse spinach leaves, then pack into a saucepan with just water left on them. Gently cook for 3 minutes until just beginning to wilt. Arrange on a warmed serving plate. Spoon pork and sauce on to centre. Trickle over coconut cream and scatter over dry-roasted peanuts.

Serves 4-6.

PORK & BAMBOO SHOOTS

PORK WITH MANGE TOUT (SNOW PEAS)

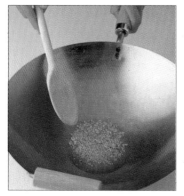

2 tablespoons vegetable oil
4 cloves garlic, very finely chopped
350 g (12 oz) lean pork, very finely chopped
115 g (4 oz) canned bamboo shoots, chopped or
   sliced
4 tablespoons peanuts, coarsely chopped
2 teaspoons Thai fish sauce
freshly ground black pepper
4 large spring onions (scallions), thinly sliced
fresh Thai holy basil sprigs, to garnish

In a wok, heat oil, add garlic and fry, stirring occasionally, for about 3 minutes until lightly coloured.

Add pork and stir-fry for 2 minutes. Add bamboo shoots and continue to stir for a further minute.

Stir in peanuts, fish sauce, plenty of black pepper and half of spring onions (scallions). Transfer to a warmed serving plate and sprinkle over remaining spring onions (scallions) and basil sprigs.

Serves 4.

4 pork chops, each weighing 175-250 g (6-8 oz),
   boned and sliced thinly lengthwise
1 teaspoon dark soy sauce
1 tablespoon yellow bean paste
2 tablespoons peanut oil
2 tablespoons Chinese rose wine or sweet sherry
2 carrots, sliced
225 g (8 oz) mange tout (snow peas)
2 cloves garlic, finely chopped
2.5 cm (1 in) piece fresh root ginger, finely chopped

Place pork in a dish. In a small bowl, mix together soy sauce, bean paste, 1 tablespoon peanut oil and rose wine or sweet sherry, then pour over pork. Turn slices to coat well and leave to marinate for 1 hour. Drain and reserve marinade. Bring a saucepan of water to a rapid boil, add carrots, mange tout (snow peas) and boil for 1 minutes. Drain and refresh under cold running water.

In a wok, heat 1 tablespoon peanut oil, fry garlic and ginger for 2-3 minutes until browned, then discard. Add pork to wok and stir-fry for 3-4 minutes until it changes colour. Add carrot and mange tout (snow peas) and stir-fry for 3 minutes, then pour in reserved marinade. Heat through for 2 minutes.

Serves 4.

BARBECUED PORK

700 g (1½ lb) pork loin, cut into long strips
115 g (4 oz/⅔ cup) brown sugar
3 tablespoons boiling water
1 tablespoon dark soy sauce
1 tablespoon oyster sauce
2 tablespoons rice wine or dry sherry
1 teaspoon sesame oil
½ teaspoon sea salt
½ teaspoon edible red food colouring, if desired
Chinese shredded lettuce, to serve

Place pork in a medium bowl. In a small bowl, stir together sugar and boiling water until sugar dissolves, then stir in remaining ingredients. Cool slightly, then pour over pork, turning pork several times to coat evenly. Leave for 8 hours turning the pork several times. Lift pork from marinade, allowing excess to drain off, reserve.

Pre-heat barbecue or grill (broiler).

Thread meat on to meat skewers and barbecue or grill (broil) for about 8 minutes until crisp and cooked, basting several times with reserved marinade.

To serve, remove the pork from the skewers, cut into bite-size pieces and serve on a bed of shredded Chinese lettuce.

Serves 4-6.

SINGAPOREAN BEEF PARCELS

2 cloves garlic, chopped
3 shallots, chopped
2 tablespoons chopped lemon grass
1 tablespoon sugar
1 tablespoon Thai fish sauce
1 tablespoon sesame oil
½ teaspoon freshly ground black pepper
450 g (1 lb) fillet steak, cut across the grain into
  thin slices about 5 cm (2 in) long
8 sheets dried rice paper, halved if large
fresh mint and coriander (cilantro) leaves
Spicy Fish Sauce, page 121

Using a pestle and mortar, pound the garlic, shallots, lemon grass and sugar to a paste.

Place paste in a mixing bowl with fish sauce, sesame oil and pepper. Blend well. Add beef and leave to marinate for at least 1 hour, the longer, the better. Meanwhile, prepare the barbecue, or preheat grill (broiler), or preheat oven to 230C (450F/Gas 8). Cook beef on barbecue for 1 minute, under grill (broiler) for 2-3 minutes, or in oven for 6-8 minutes, turning once.

To serve, dip each piece of dried rice paper in warm water to soften it, then place a slice of beef on one end of the paper, put a mint leaf and some coriander (cilantro) on top of the beef and roll into a neat parcel. Dip the parcels in the spicy fish sauce before eating.

Serves 4.

Note: This dish can also be served as a starter (appetizer), in which case it will serve 6-8.

SPICY BEEF STEW

1 tablespoon vegetable oil
2 cloves garlic, chopped
1 onion, chopped
1 stalk lemon grass, chopped
450 g (1 lb) stewing beef, cut into bite-size cubes
550 ml (20 fl oz/2½ cups) stock or water
5-6 tablespoons soy or Thai fish sauce
1 teaspoon chilli sauce
2 teaspoons Chinese five-spice powder
1 tablespoon sugar
2-3 spring onions (scallions), chopped
freshly ground black pepper
fresh coriander (cilantro) sprigs, to garnish

DRY PORK CURRY

350 g (12 oz) lean boneless pork, cut into 2 cm
  (¾ in) cubes
1 tablespoon soft brown sugar
350 g (12 oz) potatoes
225 g (8 oz) carrots
225 g (8 oz) shallots
1 tablespoon sunflower oil
2.5 cm (1 in) piece fresh root ginger, finely chopped
2 tablespoons Madras curry paste
150 ml (5 fl oz/⅔ cup) coconut milk
300 ml (10 fl oz/1¼ cups) Singaporean Chicken
  Stock, page 11
salt and freshly ground black pepper
2 tablespoons chopped fresh coriander (cilantro)

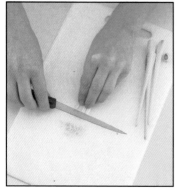

Heat oil in a clay pot or flameproof casserole and stir-fry garlic, onion, and lemon grass for about 1 minute. Add the beef and stir-fry for 2-3 minutes, or until the colour of the meat changes. Add the stock or water, bring to boil, then add the soy or fish sauce, chilli sauce, five-spice powder and sugar. Blend well, then reduce heat, cover and simmer gently for 45-50 minutes.

In a bowl, mix together the pork and brown sugar and set aside. Cut the potatoes and carrots into 2 cm (¾ in) chunks. Peel and halve the shallots.

Add spring onions (scallions), season with pepper and cook for a further 5 minutes. Garnish with coriander sprigs and serve straight from the pot, accompanied by carrots and baby corn.

Serves 4.

Variation: Substitute curry powder for the five-spice powder to make beef curry.

Heat the oil in a non-stick or well seasoned wok and stir-fry the pork, ginger and vegetables for 2-3 minutes until lightly browned. Blend curry paste with coconut milk, stock and seasoning. Stir into pork mixture and bring to the boil. Reduce heat and simmer for 40 minutes. Sprinkle with coriander (cilantro) and serve on a bed of rice.

Serves 4.

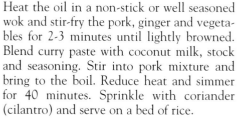

ROAST HOISIN BEEF

700 g (1½ lb) lean topside or silverside of beef
freshly ground black pepper
2 cloves garlic, finely chopped
1 cm (½ in) piece fresh root ginger, finely chopped
2 teaspoons sesame oil
4 tablespoons hoisin sauce
450 ml (16 fl oz/2 cups) Singaporean Beef Stock,
    page 11
4 carrots
1 daikon (mooli)
1 large green pepper (capsicum)
1 large yellow pepper (capsicum)
4 spring onions (scallions), shredded
spring onion (scallion) rings, to garnish

Preheat oven to 180C (350F/Gas 4). Trim any fat from the beef and place in a non-stick roasting tin (pan). Season with black pepper. Mix together the garlic, ginger, sesame oil and hoisin sauce and spread over beef. Pour half the stock into the tin (pan) and roast for 1 hour, basting occasionally to prevent drying out.

Meanwhile, peel carrots and daikon (mooli). Halve carrots and slice lengthwise. Slice daikon widthwise. Quarter and seed the peppers (capsicum). Arrange around beef, pour in the remaining stock and cook for 45-60 minutes or until tender. Drain beef and vegetables. Slice beef and serve with the vegetables, topped with shredded spring onions (scallions) and garnished with spring onion (scallion) rings.

Serves 4.

GRILLED CITRUS PORK STEAKS

4 × 115 g (4 oz) lean pork steaks, trimmed
grated rind and juice of 1 lime, 1 small lemon and 1
    small orange
1 teaspoon sesame oil
2 tablespoons dry sherry
2 tablespoons light soy sauce
1 tablespoon caster sugar
large pinch of ground white pepper
1 teaspoon cornflour (cornstarch) mixed with 2
    teaspoons water
lime, lemon and orange slices and strips of rind, to
    garnish

Score the steaks in a criss-cross pattern. Place in a shallow dish, sprinkle with citrus rinds and pour over juices.

Cover and chill for 30 minutes. Drain steaks well, reserving juices. Preheat grill (broiler). Place steaks on grill (broiler) rack and brush lightly with sesame oil. Grill (broil) for 3-4 minutes on each side until cooked through. Drain on kitchen paper and keep warm. Place reserved juices in a small saucepan with the remaining ingredients except the garnish. Bring to the boil, stirring until thickened.

Slice pork steaks and arrange on serving plates with lime, lemon and orange slices. Pour over the sauce and garnish with strips of citrus rind.

Serves 4.

GARLIC BEEF CASSEROLE

1 tablespoon groundnut (peanut) oil
450 g (1 lb) lean stewing beef, trimmed and cut into
  2 cm (¾ in) cubes
2 shallots, chopped
4 cloves garlic, thinly sliced
225 g (8 oz) carrots, sliced
175 g (6 oz) baby sweetcorn, halved lengthwise
225 g (8 oz) button mushrooms
300 ml (10 fl oz/1¼ cups) Singaporean Beef Stock,
  page 11
2 tablespoons dark soy sauce
1 tablespoon rice wine
2 teaspoons Chinese five-spice powder
2 tablespoons hoisin sauce
1 teaspoon chilli sauce

Heat oil in a non-stick or well seasoned wok and stir-fry the beef, shallots, garlic, carrots, baby sweetcorn and button mushrooms for 5 minutes. Add remaining ingredients and bring to the boil. Reduce to a simmer, cover and cook gently for 1 hour.

Remove from heat and blot surface with kitchen paper to absorb surface fat. Increase the heat and boil for 10 minutes to reduce and thicken the sauce. Serve with rice.

Serves 4.

POT-STICKER DUMPLINGS

115 g (4 oz) plain (all-purpose) flour
1 tablespoon sunflower oil
Filling:
115 g (4 oz) lean minced (ground) pork
1 cm (½ in) piece fresh root ginger, finely chopped
1 tablespoon dark soy sauce
1 tablespoon dry sherry
large pinch of ground white pepper
hoisin sauce, to serve

Place flour in a bowl and gradually add 115 ml (4 fl oz/½ cup) hot water, mixing well to form a dough. Turn out on to a floured surface and knead until smooth.

Return to the bowl, cover and set aside for 20 minutes. Mix together all the filling ingredients. Divide dough into 16 and, on a floured surface, flatten each portion into a flat round about 6 cm (2½ in) in diameter. Take one round at a time, keeping remaining rounds covered with a damp tea (dish) towel, and place a little filling in the centre. Brush edge of dough with water and bring the dough together over the filling, pinching edges together and pleating or folding them to seal. Cover with a damp tea (dish) towel while you make the remainder.

Heat the oil in a non-stick or well seasoned wok and place dumplings, flat side down, in the wok. Cook for 2 minutes until lightly browned on base. Add 150 ml (5 fl oz/⅔ cup) water, cover and cook for 10 minutes. Uncover and cook for 2 minutes. Drain and serve with a crisp salad and hoisin sauce as a dip, if liked.

Serves 4.

CURRIED BEEF

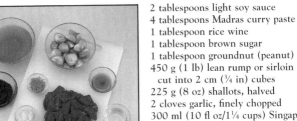

2 tablespoons light soy sauce
4 tablespoons Madras curry paste
1 tablespoon rice wine
1 tablespoon brown sugar
1 tablespoon groundnut (peanut) oil
450 g (1 lb) lean rump or sirloin steak, trimmed and
  cut into 2 cm (¾ in) cubes
225 g (8 oz) shallots, halved
2 cloves garlic, finely chopped
300 ml (10 fl oz/1¼ cups) Singaporean Beef Stock,
  page 11
1 teaspoon cornflour (cornstarch) mixed with 2
  teaspoons water
grated rind of 1 orange
4 tablespoons chopped fresh coriander (cilantro)
orange segments, to garnish

Blend together soy sauce, curry paste, rice wine and sugar and set aside. Heat oil in a non-stick or well seasoned wok and stir-fry beef, shallots and garlic for 2-3 minutes until browned. Add soy sauce mixture and stir-fry for a further minute. Pour in stock and bring to the boil. Reduce heat, cover and simmer for 1 hour until tender.

Skim any fat or scum from surface. Stir in cornflour (cornstarch) mixture, orange rind and half of the coriander. Cook, stirring, for 3-4 minutes until thickened. Sprinkle with remaining coriander (cilantro), garnish with orange segments and serve on a bed or rice.

Serves 4.

STIR-FRIED CITRUS BEEF

350 g (12 oz) lean rump or sirloin steak
2 tablespoons dark soy sauce
1 tablespoon dry sherry
2 pieces preserved mandarin rind, shredded
grated rind of 1 lime
grated rind and juice of 1 orange
1 cinnamon stick, broken
2 teaspoons cornflour (cornstarch)
2 teaspoons sunflower oil
4 spring onions (scallions), shredded
freshly ground black pepper
8 × 25 g (1 oz) clusters vermicelli egg noodles
lime and orange slices and strips of rind, to garnish

Trim any fat from the beef and cut beef into 2 cm (¾ in) pieces. Place in a bowl.
Add the soy sauce, sherry, mandarin rind, lime rind, orange rind and juice, cinnamon stick and cornflour (cornstarch) and mix well. Cover and chill for 30 minutes. Heat oil in a non-stick or well seasoned wok and stir-fry beef mixture for 2-3 minutes. Add the spring onions (scallions) and seasoning and simmer for a further 2-3 minutes until the beef is tender. Discard cinnamon stick.

Meanwhile, bring a large saucepan of water to the boil, add noodle clusters, reduce heat and simmer gently for 2-3 minutes, taking care they retain their shape. Remove from the pan with a slotted spoon, drain well and arrange on serving plates. Top with the beef mixture, garnish and serve with steamed carrots.

Serves 4.

SPICED BEEF

450 g (1 lb) lean beef fillet
1 tablespoon sunflower oil
1 clove garlic, finely chopped
1 cm (½ in) piece fresh root ginger, finely chopped
4 spring onions (scallions), finely chopped
1 tablespoon hoisin sauce
1 teaspoon Szechuan peppercorns, toasted and
  ground
115 g (4 oz) Szechuan preserved vegetables
1 teaspoon caster sugar
shredded spring onions (scallions), to garnish

Trim any fat and silver skin from the beef.
Cut beef into very thin slices.

Heat oil in a non-stick or well seasoned wok
and stir-fry the beef, garlic, ginger and spring
onions (scallions) for 1 minute until the beef
is browned.

Add remaining ingredients except the garnish and stir-fry for a further 3-4 minutes
until beef is just cooked through. Garnish
with shredded spring onions (scallions) and
serve with rice.

Serves 4.

BEEF WITH OYSTER SAUCE

450 g (1 lb) lean rump or sirloin steak
25 g (1 oz) dried Chinese mushrooms, soaked in hot
  water for 20 minutes
225 g (8 oz) oyster mushrooms
1 tablespoon light soy sauce
1 tablespoon dry sherry
freshly ground black pepper
2 tablespoons oyster sauce
1 tablespoon sunflower oil
2 tablespoons chopped fresh chives, to garnish

Trim any fat from steak and cut into 5 mm
(¼ in) strips. Drain the soaked mushrooms,
squeezing out excess water. Discard stems
and slice caps. Slice oyster mushrooms.

Mix together soy sauce, sherry, black pepper
and oyster sauce and set aside. Heat the oil
in a non-stick or well seasoned wok and stir-
fry beef and mushrooms for 2-3 minutes until
beef is browned.

Stir soy sauce mixture into beef and stir-fry
for a further 2-3 minutes until beef is tender.
Garnish with chives and serve on a bed of
noodles with freshly cooked vegetables.

Serves 4.

BEEF & SEAFOOD FONDUE

225 g (8 oz) beef fillet, sliced paper thin
115 g (4 oz) firm white fish fillet, thinly sliced
115 g (4 oz) cleaned prepared squid
6 raw peeled prawns (shrimp), cut in half lengthwise
1 tomato and 1 onion, thinly sliced
freshly ground black pepper
1 tablespoon sesame oil
2 teaspoons vegetable oil
1 clove garlic, chopped
2 shallots, chopped
1 tablespoon each tomato paste and sugar
1 teaspoon salt
2 tablespoons rice vinegar
685 ml (24-fl oz/3 cups) stock or water

FONDUE ACCOMPANIMENTS:
55 g (2 oz) bean thread vermicelli, soaked then cut
  into short lengths
6-8 Chinese dried mushrooms, soaked and each cut
  in half or quartered
2 cakes bean curd, cut into small cubes
115 g (4 oz) bok choy (Chinese cabbage), cut into
  small pieces
dried rice paper or lettuce leaves
fresh mint and coriander leaves
Spicy Fish Sauce, page 121

Arrange the vermicelli, mushrooms, bean curd cubes and bok choy on a serving platter in separate sections.

Arrange the beef and seafood on a platter in separate sections. Place tomato and onion slices in the centre and sprinkle pepper and sesame oil all over them. Set aside while you prepare the broth.

If using large sheets of rice paper, cut in half; if using lettuce leaves, separate them, and place on a serving dish. Place spicy sauce in individual small saucers for dipping. To serve, bring boiling broth in the hot pot or fondue to the table; each person picks up a slice of beef or some seafood with vegetables and dips them into the broth to be cooked very briefly - usually no more than 1 minute.

Heat vegetable oil in a saucepan and stir-fry the garlic and shallots for about 30 seconds, then add the tomato paste, sugar, salt and rice vinegar. Blend well, then add the stock or water, bring to boil and transfer to a Chinese hot pot or fondue.

Meanwhile, dip a piece of rice paper in hot water to soften it. Quickly remove the food from the broth and place in the middle of the rice paper or a lettuce leaf, add a few mint and coriander leaves, then fold over to make into a neat parcel. Dip the parcel in the spicy fish sauce before eating.

Serves 4-6.

DRY-FRIED BEEF STRIPS

2 tablespoons sesame oil
450 g (1 lb) rump or sirloin steak, cut crosswise into
    julienne strips
2 tablespoons rice wine or dry sherry
1 tablespoon light soy sauce
2 cloves garlic, finely chopped
1 cm (½ in) piece fresh root ginger, finely chopped
1 tablespoon Chinese chilli bean paste (sauce)
2 teaspoons sugar
1 carrot, cut into julienne strips
2 stalks celery, cut into julienne strips
2-3 spring onions (scallions), thinly sliced
½ teaspoon ground Szechuan peppercorns
cucumber matchsticks, to garnish

Heat the wok until very hot. Add the oil and swirl to coat wok. Add beef and stir-fry for 15 seconds to quickly seal meat. Add 1 table-spoon rice wine or sherry and stir-fry for 1-2 minutes until beef is browned. Pour off and reserve any excess liquid and continue stir-frying until beef is dry.

Stir in soy sauce, garlic, ginger, chilli bean paste, sugar, remaining rice wine or sherry and any reserved cooking juices and stir to blend well. Add carrot, celery, spring onions (scallions) and ground Szechuan pepper and stir-fry until the vegetables begin to soften and all the liquid is absorbed. Garnish with cucumber matchsticks and serve with rice and wild rice.

Serves 4.

MANGO BEEF WITH CASHEWS

450 g (1 lb) lean rump or sirloin steak
1 clove garlic, finely chopped
1 tablespoon light soy sauce
1 tablespoon rice wine
1 teaspoon cornflour (cornstarch)
salt and freshly ground black pepper
2 ripe mangoes
1 tablespoon sunflower oil
2 tablespoons chopped fresh coriander (cilantro)
25 g (1 oz/½ cup) unsalted cashew nuts, coarsely
    crushed

Trim any fat from the beef and cut into 5 mm (¼ in) strips.

Place in a bowl and mix with garlic, soy sauce, rice wine, cornflour (cornstarch) and seasoning. Cover and chill for 30 minutes. Peel the mangoes and slice flesh off the large flat stone in the centre of each mango. Cut flesh into thick, even slices, reserving a few small strips for garnish.

Heat oil in a non-stick or well seasoned wok and stir-fry beef mixture for 3-4 minutes until beef is browned all over. Stir in sliced mango and cook gently for 2-3 minutes to heat through. Sprinkle with chopped corian-der (cilantro) and crushed cashews, garnish with reserved mango and serve on a bed of rice.

Serves 4.

CHINESE SAUSAGE STIR-FRY

GINGER BEEF WITH PINEAPPLE

2 tablespoons sesame or vegetable oil
225 g (8 oz) Chinese sausage or Italian-style
 sausage, cut diagonally into thin slices
1 onion, cut in half lengthwise and sliced
1 red pepper (capsicum), diced
115 g (4 oz) baby sweetcorn
2 courgettes (zucchini), thinly sliced
115 g (4 oz) mange tout (snow peas)
8 spring onions (scallions), cut into 2.5 cm (1 in)
 pieces
25 g (1 oz) beansprouts, rinsed and drained
25 g (1 oz/¼ cup) cashew nuts or peanuts
2 tablespoons soy sauce
3 tablespoons dry sherry or rice wine

450 g (1 lb) lean rump or sirloin steak
salt and freshly ground black pepper
1 tablespoon ginger wine
2.5 cm (1 in) piece fresh root ginger, finely chopped
1 clove garlic, finely chopped
1 teaspoon cornflour (cornstarch)
225 g (8 oz) fresh pineapple
1 tablespoon sunflower oil
2 red peppers (capsicum), thinly sliced
4 spring onions (cornstarch), chopped
2 tablespoons light soy sauce
1 piece stem ginger in syrup, drained and thickly
 sliced

Heat the wok until hot. Add sesame or vegetable oil and swirl to coat wok. Add sausage slices and stir-fry for 3-4 minutes until browned and cooked. Add onion, pepper and sweetcorn and stir-fry for 3 minutes. Add courgettes (zucchini), mange tout (snow peas) and spring onions (scallions) and stir-fry for a further 2 minutes.

Trim any visible fat from the beef and cut into 5mm (¼ in) strips. Place in a bowl and season. Add the ginger wine, chopped ginger, chopped garlic and the cornflour (cornstarch) and mix well. Cover and chill for 30 minutes. Meanwhile, peel and core the pineapple and cut into 2.5 cm (1 in) cubes.

Stir in the beansprouts and nuts and stir-fry for 1-2 minutes. Add soy sauce and dry sherry or rice wine and stir-fry for 1 minute until vegetables are tender but still crisp and sausage slices completely cooked through. Serve with rice noodles.

Serves 4.

Heat oil in a non-stick or well seasoned wok, add beef mixture and stir-fry for 1-2 minutes until beef is browned all over. Add peppers (capsicum) and stir-fry for a further minute. Add spring onions (scallions), pineapple and soy sauce and simmer gently for 2-3 minutes, to heat through. Sprinkle with stem ginger and serve on a bed of noodles.

Serves 4.

STIR-FRIED BEEF STEAK

STIR-FRIED BEEF WITH LEEKS

225 g (8 oz) beef steak, cut into small, thin slices,
    about 2.5 cm (1 in) square
¼ teaspoon freshly ground black pepper
1 teaspoon sugar
1 tablespoon fish sauce
2 tablespoons vegetable oil
1 clove garlic, chopped
1 small onion, sliced
1 green pepper (capsicum), cored and cut into cubes
115 g (4 oz) sliced bamboo shoots, drained
1 firm tomato, cut into 8 wedges
2 spring onions (scallions), cut into short lengths
2 tablespoons soy or oyster sauce
2 teaspoons cornflour (cornstarch)

450 g (1 lb) lean rump or sirloin steak
1 tablespoon dark soy sauce
1 teaspoon sesame oil
freshly ground black pepper
1 tablespoon dry sherry
2 teaspoons cornflour (cornstarch)
450 g (1 lb) leeks
115 g (4 oz) spring onions (scallions)
2 teaspoons sunflower oil
2 teaspoons caster sugar
150 ml (5 fl oz/⅔ cup) Singaporean Beef Stock, page
  11
2 tablespoons chopped fresh chives
fresh chives, to garnish

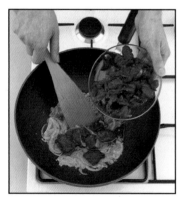

Mix beef with black pepper, sugar and fish sauce and leave to marinate for 15-20 minutes. Heat oil in a wok or frying pan (skillet) and stir-fry garlic and onion for about 1 minutes. Add the beef and stir-fry for 1 minute.

Trim any fat from the beef and cut into 2 cm (¾ in) pieces. Place in a bowl and mix in soy sauce, sesame oil, black pepper, sherry and cornflour (cornstarch). Cover and chill for 30 minutes. Trim leeks and discard any coarse outer leaves. Slice thinly and wash well to remove any soil. Trim and shred the spring onions (scallions).

Add the green pepper (capsicum), bamboo shoots, tomato and spring onions (scallions). Continue stir-frying for 2-3 minutes, then blend in the soy or oyster sauce. Mix the cornflour (cornstarch) with 1 tablespoon water and stir into mixture. Cook, stirring, until thickened. Serve with rice noodles.

Serves 4.

Heat oil in a non-stick or well seasoned wok and stir-fry beef mixture for 1-2 minutes until beef is browned. Add leeks, spring onions (scallions) and sugar and stir-fry for 3-4 minutes until browned. Pour in the stock and simmer for 5 minutes, stirring occasionally, until thickened. Stir in chopped chives, garnish with chives and serve with noodles.

Serves 4.

BEEF WITH WATER CHESTNUTS

BEEF CURRY

450 g (1 lb) lean rump or sirloin steak
1 tablespoon dark soy sauce
1 tablespoon dry sherry
1 teaspoon chilli sauce
2 teaspoons brown sugar
2 teaspoons cornflour (cornstarch)
225 g (8 oz) broccoli
115 g (4 oz) canned water chestnuts, drained
1 tablespoon sunflower oil
salt and freshly ground black pepper
strips of fresh red chilli, to garnish

Trim any fat from the beef and cut into 2 cm
(¾ in) pieces.

2 tablespoons vegetable oil
3 tablespoons Thai red curry paste
350 g (12 oz) lean beef, cut into cubes
1 stalk lemon grass, finely chopped
115 g (4 oz) long beans, or green beans, cut into
    4 cm (1½ in) lengths
about 8 pieces dried Chinese black mushrooms,
    soaked, drained and chopped
3 tablespoons roasted peanuts
1 fresh green chilli, deseeded and chopped
1 tablespoon fish sauce
2 teaspoons crushed palm sugar
15 fresh Thai mint leaves

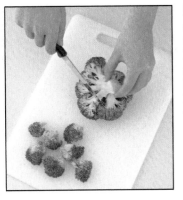

Place beef in a bowl, and mix with soy sauce,
sherry, chilli sauce, sugar and cornflour
(cornstarch). Cover and chill for 30 minutes.
Meanwhile, cut the broccoli into small flowerets. Bring a small saucepan of water to the
boil and cook the broccoli for 3 minutes.
Drain and rinse in cold water. Halve the
water chestnuts.

In a wok, heat oil, add curry paste and stir for
3 minutes. Add beef and lemon grass and
stir-fry for 5 minutes. Add beans and mushrooms, stir-fry for 3 minutes, then stir in
peanuts and chilli.

Heat the oil in a non-stick or well seasoned
wok. Add the beef mixture and stir-fry for 2-
3 minutes. Add the broccoli and water
chestnuts, season and stir-fry for 3 minutes.
Garnish with strips of red chilli and serve
with noodles.

Serves 4.

Stir for 1 minute, then stir in 4 tablespoons
water, the fish sauce and sugar and cook for
about 2 minutes until beans are tender but
crisp. Transfer to a warmed serving dish and
scatter over mint leaves.

Serves 3-4.

CURRIED COCONUT BEEF

1.5 litres (53 fl oz/6⅔ cups) coconut milk
4 fresh bay leaves
1.4 kg (3 lb) braising steak, cut into 5 cm (2 in) cubes
Curry paste:
6 shallots, chopped
6 cloves garlic, smashed
6 fresh red chillies, cored, deseeded and chopped
7.5 cm (3 in) piece galangal, chopped
2 stalks lemon grass, chopped
2.5 cm (1 in) piece cinnamon
12 whole cloves
1 teaspoon ground turmeric

Mix all curry paste ingredients in a blender. Add a little coconut milk, if necessary.

In a saucepan, combine curry paste and coconut milk. Add bay leaves and bring to a boil over high heat, stirring occasionally. Lower heat to medium and cook sauce, stirring occasionally, for 15 minutes.

Stir in beef. Simmer, uncovered, stirring occasionally, for 2 hours. Reduce heat to very low and cook beef for a further 1½-2 hours until sauce is quite thick. Stir frequently to prevent sticking. Skim fat and oil from surface. Serve with boiled rice.

Serves 8.

'DRY' BEEF WITH COCONUT

4 tablespoons vegetable oil
6 shallots, finely chopped
3 cloves garlic, finely chopped
1 fresh red chilli, cored, deseeded and finely chopped
700 g (1½ lb) lean beef, thinly sliced and cut into
   1 cm (½ in) strips
1 tablespoon light brown sugar
1½ teaspoons ground cumin
1 teaspoon ground coriander
squeeze of lime juice
salt
½ fresh coconut, grated, or 225 g (8 oz/2⅔ cups)
   desiccated (unsweetened shredded) coconut

In a wok or sauté pan, heat 1 tablespoon oil over medium heat. Add shallots, garlic and chilli and fry for about 5 minutes, stirring occasionally, until softened but not browned. Add beef, sugar, cumin, coriander, lime juice, salt to taste and 150 ml (5 fl oz/⅔ cup) water. Cover pan tightly and simmer gently for 30 minutes, stirring occasionally.

Uncover pan, stir in coconut until all the liquid has been absorbed. Stir in the remaining oil and continue stirring until the coconut begins to brown.

Serves 6.

BEEF IN CHILLI SAUCE

BOILED BEEF WITH CHILLIES

8 dried red chillies, cored, deseeded and chopped
2 small onions, chopped
5 cm (2 in) piece of fresh root ginger, chopped
700 g (1½ lb) lean beef, cut into bite-size pieces
1 tablespoon each ground coriander and cumin
1 tablespoon tomato ketchup (catsup)
2 teaspoons each turmeric and paprika
2 tablespoons vegetable oil
2 cloves garlic, crushed
2.5 cm (1 in) stick cinnamon
seeds from 3 cardamom pods, crushed
½ star anise
sugar and salt
1 onion, sliced into thick rings

450 g (1 lb) rump steak, cut into paper thin slices
8 lettuce leaves, diced
½ teaspoon ground Szechuan peppercorns
1 clove garlic, finely chopped
Sauce:
2 tablespoons peanut oil
4 dried red chillies, crushed
1 teaspoon ground Szechuan peppercorns
1 tablespoon fermented black beans
4 spring onions (scallions), coarsely chopped
2 cloves garlic, crushed
1 cm (½ in) piece fresh root ginger, finely chopped
1 tablespoon hot bean paste

Put chillies in a small blender. Add 4 tablespoons hot water and leave until slightly softened. Add half of small onions and half of ginger to blender and mix to a paste. Put beef in a large bowl. Add spice paste from blender, coriander, cumin, tomato ketchup (catsup), turmeric and paprika. Stir together. Cover and leave for at least 1 hour to marinate.

To make the sauce, in a wok, heat oil and briskly fry chillies and pepper for 30 seconds, then add black beans and cook for a further 30 seconds. Add spring onions (scallions), garlic, ginger and bean paste, and continue to fry for 5-6 minutes. Stir in 115 ml (4 fl oz/½ cup) water and bring to the boil, then remove from the heat.

In a wok, heat oil over medium-high heat. Add remaining onion and ginger, and the garlic. Fry, stirring, for 3 minutes until lightly browned. Stir in next 3 ingredients for 1 minute. Add meat and marinade and cook over medium-high heat, stirring, for 5 minutes. Add 350 ml (12 fl oz/1½ cups) water, and sugar and salt to taste. Cover pan. Simmer very gently for 1¼ hours or until beef is tender. Stir occasionally. Add onion rings and cook for 3-5 minutes or until soft.

Serves 4-6.

To prepare the beef, bring a large saucepan of water to a rapid boil. Add beef and boil for 2 minutes until it just changes colour. Drain well. Re-heat sauce in the wok, add beef, stir for 3 minutes, then add the lettuce. Serve immediately sprinkled with Szechuan peppercorns and finely chopped garlic.

Serves 4.

NOODLES & RICE

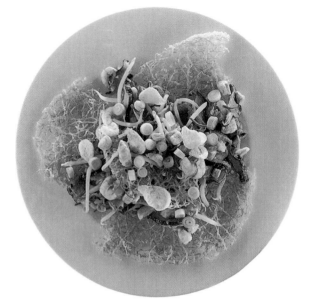

CRISPY NOODLES

175 g (6 oz) rice vermicelli
6 pieces dried Chinese black mushrooms
115 g (4 oz) lean pork
115 g (4 oz) chicken breast
vegetable oil for deep frying
2 eggs
4 cloves garlic, finely chopped
3 shallots, thinly sliced
1 fresh red chilli, deseeded and sliced
1 fresh green chilli, deseeded and sliced
6 tablespoons lime juice
1 tablespoon Thai fish sauce
1 tablespoon crushed palm sugar
45 g (1½ oz) cooked peeled shrimps
115 g (4 oz) beansprouts
3 spring onions (scallions), thickly sliced

Soak vermicelli in water for 20 minutes, then drain and set aside. Soak mushrooms in water for 20 minutes, then drain, chop and set aside. Cook pork and chicken into 2.5 cm (1 in) strips or small dice. Set aside.

For garnish, heat 2 teaspoons oil in a wok. In a small bowl, beat eggs with 2 tablespoons water, then drip small amounts in batches in tear shapes on to wok. Cook for 1½-2 minutes until set. Remove using a fish slice or thin spatula. Set aside.

Add more oil to wok until there is sufficient for deep frying. Heat to 190C (375F). Add vermicelli in batches and fry until puffed, light golden brown and crisp. Transfer to absorbent kitchen paper. Set aside.

Pour off oil leaving 3 tablespoons. Add garlic and shallots and cook, stirring occasionally, until lightly browned. Add pork, stir-fry for 1 minute, then mix in chicken and stir for 2 minutes. Stir in chillies, mushrooms, lime juice, fish sauce and sugar.

Bubble until liquid becomes very lightly syrupy. Add shrimps, beansprouts and noodles, tossing to coat with sauce without breaking up noodles. Serve with spring onions (scallions) scattered over and garnished with egg 'tears'.

Serves 4.

FRIED NOODLES WITH CRAB

4-6 dried Chinese mushrooms
350 g (12 oz) dried Chinese egg noodles
3 tablespoons vegetable oil
1 small onion, finely chopped
3 cloves garlic, finely chopped
2 cm (¾ in) piece of fresh root ginger, grated
115 g (4 oz) boneless, skinless chicken breast, cut
   into strips.
115 g (4 oz) raw peeled medium prawns (shrimp)
115 g (4 oz) choi sum, torn into shreds
oyster sauce
115 g (4 oz/½ cup) cooked crabmeat
egg strips made from 1 egg (see page 101) and 1
   spring onion (scallion), including some green,
   sliced, to garnish

Soak mushrooms in hot water for 15 minutes. Strain, reserving liquid. Slice caps and discard stalks. Set aside. Cook noodles in a large saucepan of boiling water according to package instructions. Drain, rinse and drain again. Set aside. In a wok or large frying pan (skillet), heat oil over medium heat. Add onion, garlic and ginger and cook for about 4 minutes until softened but not brown. Increase heat to high. Add chicken and stir-fry for 2-3 minutes until opaque. Add prawns (shrimp) and stir-fry for 1-1½ minutes until just turning pink.

Quickly stir in the choi sum, then add the noodles and mushrooms, plus enough of the soaking liquid to prevent the dish being dry. Add oyster sauce to taste. Transfer noodle mixture to a deep, warm plate. Top with crab and garnish with egg strips and spring onion (scallion).

Serves 3-4.

VEGETARIAN FRIED NOODLES

2 tablespoons vegetable oil
1 clove garlic, chopped
1 onion, sliced
2-3 small red chillies, deseeded and shredded
1 carrot, thinly shredded
225 g (8 oz) bean sprouts
salt and freshly ground black pepper
225 g (8 oz) rice vermicelli, soaked in hot water for
   5 minutes, drained and cut into short lengths
2 tablespoons soy sauce
shredded spring onions (scallions), to garnish

Heat oil in a wok or frying pan (skillet) and stir-fry garlic and onion for 1 minute until opaque.

Add the chillies and carrot shreds, continue stirring for 2 minutes, then add the bean sprouts with salt and pepper. Blend well and stir-fry for 2 more minutes.

Add the rice vermicelli with the soy sauce, mix and toss, then cook for 2-3 minutes. Garnish with shredded spring onions (scallions) and serve at once.

Serves 4.

CRAB & AUBERGINE NOODLES

225 g (8 oz/1 cup) brown and white crabmeat
175 g (6 oz) dried egg thread noodles
3 tablespoons vegetable oil
1 aubergine (eggplant), about 225 g (8 oz), cut into
about 5 × 5 mm (2 × ¼ in) strips
2 cloves garlic, very finely chopped
1 cm (½ in) slice galangal, finely chopped
1 fresh green chilli, deseeded and finely chopped
6 spring onions (scallions), sliced
1 tablespoon Thai fish sauce
2 teaspoons lime juice
1½ tablespoons chopped fresh coriander (cilantro)
leaves
fresh coriander (cilantro), to garnish

NOODLES WITH BROCCOLI

450 g (1 lb) wet rice noodles
225 g (8 oz) broccoli
2 tablespoons vegetable oil
3 cloves garlic, finely chopped
225 g (8 oz) lean pork, finely chopped
4 tablespoons roasted peanuts, chopped
2 teaspoons Thai fish sauce
¼ teaspoon crushed palm sugar
1 fresh red chilli, deseeded and cut into thin slivers,
to garnish

In a bowl, well mash brown crabmeat. Roughly mash white meat. Set aside.

Add noodles to a saucepan of boiling salted water and cook for about 4 minutes until just tender. Drain well. Meanwhile, in a wok, heat 2 tablespoons oil, add aubergine (eggplant) and stir-fry for about 5 minutes until evenly well coloured. Using a slotted spoon, transfer to absorbent kitchen paper; set aside.

Remove wrapping from noodles and immediately cut into 1 cm (½ in) strips; set aside. Cut broccoli diagonally into 5 cm (2 in) wide pieces and cook in a saucepan of boiling salted water for 2 minutes. Drain, refresh under cold running water and drain well; set aside.

Add remaining oil to wok, heat, then one by one stir in garlic, galangal, chilli, finally spring onions (scallions). Add noodles, toss together for 1 minute, then toss in crab meats and aubergine (eggplant). Sprinkle over fish sauce, lime juice and coriander (cilantro), and toss to mix. Garnish with coriander (cilantro) sprig.

Serves 3.

In a wok, heat oil, add garlic and fry, stirring occasionally, until golden. Using a slotted spoon, transfer to absorbent kitchen paper; set aside. Add pork to wok and stir-fry for 2 minutes. Add noodles, stir quickly, then add broccoli and peanuts and stir-fry for 2 minutes. Stir in fish sauce, sugar and 3 tablespoons water. Stir briefly and serve garnished with reserved garlic and chilli slivers.

Serves 4.

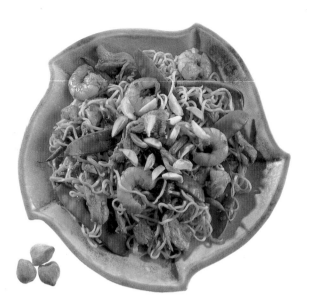

CHICKEN & PRAWN NOODLES

225 g (8 oz) boneless, skinless chicken breast, very
  thinly sliced
225 g (8 oz) raw prawns (shrimp), peeled and deveined
5 tablespoons groundnut oil
1 tablespoon sesame oil
1 teaspoon ground coriander
pinch of Chinese five-spice powder
115 g (4 oz) thin dried Chinese egg noodles
55 g (2 oz) each mange tout (snow peas) and French
  (green) beans, halved
2 cloves garlic, finely crushed
1½ teaspoons grated fresh root ginger
2 fresh red chillies, cored, deseeded and finely chopped
1 tablespoon dark soy sauce
1 tablespoon lime juice
2 tablespoons chopped fresh coriander (cilantro)
toasted candlenuts or cashew nuts, to garnish

Put chicken and prawns (shrimp) into a
non-reactive bowl. Stir together 1 tablespoon groundnut oil, 1 teaspoon sesame oil,
ground coriander and five-spice powder.
Pour over chicken and prawns (shrimp). Stir
until evenly coated. Cook noodles according
to package instructions. Meanwhile, in a
wok or sauté pan, heat 2 tablespoons groundnut oil. Add chicken and prawns (shrimp)
and stir-fry for 2 minutes. Using a slotted
spoon, transfer to paper towels to drain. Add
vegetables to pan and stir-fry for 1 minute.

Transfer chicken and prawns (shrimp) to
serving bowl. Keep warm. In a small pan,
heat remaining groundnut oil and sesame
oil. Add garlic, ginger and chillies and fry
gently for 4-5 minutes until softened but not
coloured. Whisk in soy sauce, lime juice and
2 tablespoons water. Bring to a boil then
remove from heat. Drain noodles and
quickly toss with chicken and garlic mix-
tures. Serve warm or cold sprinkled with
chopped coriander and toasted nuts.

Serves 4.

COCONUT NOODLES

225 g (8 oz) wholewheat linguini, tagliatelle or
  spaghetti
55 ml (2 fl oz/¼ cup) groundnut oil
115 g (4 oz) shiitake or oyster mushrooms
1 red pepper (capsicum), thinly sliced
½ small Chinese cabbage, thinly shredded
115 g (4 oz) mange tout (snow peas), thinly sliced
4-6 spring onions (scallions), thinly sliced
175 ml (6 fl oz/¾ cup) unsweetened coconut milk
2 tablespoons rice wine or dry sherry
1 tablespoon soy sauce
1 tablespoon oyster sauce
1 teaspoon Chinese chilli sauce
3 teaspoons cornflour (cornstarch) dissolved in 2
  tablespoons water
8 tablespoons chopped fresh mint or coriander (cilantro)
fresh mint or coriander (cilantro) sprigs, to garnish

In a large saucepan of boiling water, cook the
noodles according to the packet directions.
Drain and toss with 1 tablespoon of groundnut oil. Heat the wok until hot. Add the
remaining oil and swirl to coat wok. Add
mushrooms, pepper (capsicum) and Chinese
cabbage and stir-fry for 2-3 minutes until
vegetables begin to soften. Stir in reserved
noodles, mange tout (snow peas) and spring
onions (scallions) and stir-fry for 1 minute to
combine.

Slowly pour in coconut milk, rice wine or
sherry, soy sauce, oyster sauce and chilli
sauce and bring to simmering point. Stir the
cornflour (cornstarch) mixture and, pushing
ingredients to one side, stir into the wok.
Stir to combine liquid ingredients well, then
stir in chopped mint or coriander (cilantro)
and toss to coat well. Stir-fry for 2-3 minutes
until heated through. Serve hot, garnished
with sprigs of mint or coriander (cilantro).

Serves 4.

PORK & PRAWN NOODLES

SESAME NOODLE SALAD

200 g (7 oz) bean thread noodles
6 dried Chinese black mushrooms
2 tablespoons vegetable oil
350 g (12 oz) lean pork, very finely chopped
115 g (4 oz) cooked peeled large prawns (shrimp)
3 red shallots, finely chopped
4 spring onions (scallions), including some green, sliced
3 slim inner celery stalks, thinly sliced
55 g (2 oz) dried shrimps
2 tablespoons Thai fish sauce
5 tablespoons lime juice
1½ teaspoons crushed palm sugar
2 fresh red chillies, deseeded and chopped
15 g (½ oz/½ cup) fresh coriander (cilantro) leaves, chopped
whole cooked prawns (shrimp) and fresh coriander (cilantro), to garnish

200 g (7 oz) fine rice noodles
1 carrot
4 spring onions (scallions), sliced
1 tablespoon toasted sesame seeds
fresh coriander (cilantro) sprigs, to garnish
Sesame dressing:
5 teaspoons sesame paste
5 teaspoons sesame oil
5 teaspoons soy sauce
2 tablespoon rice vinegar
1 teaspoon sugar
1 teaspoon grated fresh root ginger
salt and freshly ground black pepper

Soak noodles as directed on package, until soft. Drain and set aside.

Soak noodles in cold water for 15 minutes. Soak mushrooms in water for 30 minutes. Drain and chop. In a wok, heat oil, add pork and stir-fry for 2-3 minutes until cooked through. Using a slotted spoon, transfer to absorbent kitchen paper. Add noodles to a saucepan of boiling water and boil for 5 minutes. Drain well and set aside.

Cut carrot into 2.5 cm (1 in) long matchsticks. Blanch in boiling water for 1 minute. Drain, rinse in cold water, drain again and set aside.

Cut each prawn into 3 and place in a bowl. Add shallots, spring onions (scallions), celery, mushrooms, noodles, pork and dried shrimps; toss together. In a small bowl, mix together fish sauce, lime juice and sugar. Pour into bowl, add coriander (cilantro) leaves and toss ingredients together. Serve garnished with whole prawns (shrimp) and coriander (cilantro) sprigs.

To make sesame dressing, in a large bowl, mix together sesame paste, sesame oil, soy sauce, rice vinegar, sugar, ginger and salt and pepper. Add noodles and toss to coat thoroughly. Stir in carrot and spring onions (scallions). Sprinkle with sesame seeds, garnish with coriander (cilantro) sprigs and serve at once.

Serves 4.

Serves 6.

Variation: Add cooked, peeled prawns (shrimp) or diced ham before serving.

COLD SPICY NOODLES

SPICED RICE

450 g (1 lb) soba (buckwheat) noodles or
  wholewheat spaghetti
2 tablespoons sesame oil
2 cloves garlic, finely chopped
1 green pepper (capsicum), thinly sliced
115 g (4 oz) mange tout (snow peas), sliced
115 g (4 oz) daikon (mooli), thinly sliced
2 tablespoons light soy sauce
3 teaspoons cider vinegar
3-6 teaspoons Chinese chilli paste or sauce
2 teaspoons sugar
70 ml (2½ fl oz/½ cup) peanut butter or sesame paste
8-10 spring onions (scallions), thinly sliced
toasted chopped peanuts or toasted sesame seeds, to
  garnish
cucumber matchsticks, to serve (optional)

5 cm (2 in) cinnamon stick
1 tablespoon coriander seeds, lightly crushed
seeds from 1 green cardamom pod, lightly crushed
2 whole star anise
1 small onion, chopped
2 garlic cloves, chopped
2 cm (¾ in) piece of fresh root ginger, chopped
1 tablespoon vegetable oil
225 g (8 oz/1 cup) long-grain rice, rinsed
1 teaspoon dark soy sauce
1 tablespoon candlenuts or cashew nuts
2 tablespoons raisins

Put cinnamon, coriander and cardamom seeds and star anise in a saucepan.

In a large saucepan of boiling water, cook noodles or spaghetti according to package directions. Drain and rinse well. Drain again and toss with 1 tablespoon sesame oil. Set aside. Heat the wok until very hot. Add remaining sesame oil and swirl to coat. Add garlic and stir-fry for 5-10 seconds. Add pepper (capsicum), mange tout (snow peas) and daikon. Stir-fry for 1 minute until fragrant and brightly coloured.

Add 850 ml (30 fl oz/3¾ cups) water. Simmer uncovered until reduced to 450 ml (16 fl oz/2 cups). Set aside to cool. Put onion, garlic and ginger in a blender and mix to a paste, adding a little of spiced water if necessary. In a saucepan, heat oil over medium-high heat. Add paste and fry for 3-4 minutes, stirring occasionally.

Stir in soy sauce, vinegar, chilli paste and sauce, sugar, peanut butter or sesame paste and 55 ml (2 fl oz/¼ cup) hot water. Remove from heat. Stir until peanut butter or sesame paste is diluted and smooth, adding a little more water, if necessary. Add reserved noodles and toss to coat. Turn into a large shallow bowl and allow to cool. Before serving, toss again, adding spring onions (scallions) and sprinkling with peanuts or sesame seeds. Serve with cucumber, if wished.

Serves 4-6.

Stir in rice. Strain in spiced water, add soy sauce and bring to a boil. Stir, cover and simmer until rice is tender and liquid has been absorbed. Add nuts and raisins and fluff up rice with chopsticks or a fork.

Serves 4 as a side dish.

GREEN RICE

SHRIMP NOODLES

300 g (10 oz/1¼ cups) long-grain white rice, rinsed.
800 ml (28 fl oz/3½ cups) Vegetable Stock, page 12
225 g (8 oz) small broccoli flowerets
225 g (8 oz) fresh spinach, tough stalks removed
1 tablespoon groundnut (peanut) oil
2 cloves garlic, finely chopped
1 fresh green chilli, deseeded and chopped
1 bunch spring onions (scallions), finely chopped
225 g (8 oz/2 cups) frozen peas
2 tablespoons light soy sauce
salt and freshly ground black pepper
4 tablespoons chopped fresh chives
fresh chives, to garnish

225 g (8 oz) vermicelli rice noodles
25 g (1 oz) dried Chinese mushrooms, soaked in hot
  water for 20 minutes
2 teaspoons chilli oil
4 spring onions (scallions), shredded
225 g (8 oz) cooked, peeled shrimps or small
  prawns, thawed and dried, if frozen
225 g (8 oz/2 cups) frozen peas
1 tablespoon oyster sauce
grated rind of 1 lemon
1 egg, lightly beaten

Bring a large saucepan of water to the boil.
Turn off heat and add noodles. Loosen with
2 forks and let soak for 3 minutes.

Place rice and stock in a large saucepan,
bring to the boil, reduce heat and simmer
gently for 25 minutes until the rice is cooked
and the liquid has been absorbed. Blanch the
broccoli in a saucepan of boiling water for 2
minutes. Drain and set aside. Blanch the
spinach in a saucepan of boiling water for a
few seconds until just wilted. Drain well,
shred and set aside.

Drain noodles well and rinse in cold water.
Drain mushrooms and squeeze out excess
water. Discard stems and slice caps. Heat half
the chilli oil in a non-stick or well seasoned
wok and stir-fry minutes, spring onions (scallions), shrimps or prawns and peas for 2
minutes. Add oyster sauce, lemon rind and
noodles and stir-fry for 2 minutes. Keep
warm.

Heat oil in a non-stick or well seasoned wok
and stir-fry garlic, chilli, spring onions (scallions) and broccoli for 1 minute. Add
cooked rice, spinach, frozen peas and soy
sauce. Season well and cook gently for 5
minutes. Stir in chopped chives. Garnish
with chives.

Serves 4.

Heat remaining oil in a small non-stick frying pan (skillet) and cook egg for 1-2
minutes on each side until set. Slide on to a
plate, roll up and cut into thin rounds.
Garnish noodles with rounds of egg and
serve immediately.

Serves 4.

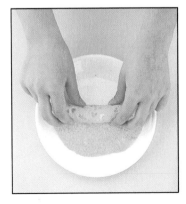

RICE WITH LEMON GRASS

500 ml (18 fl oz/2¼ cups) coconut milk
2 stalks lemon grass, bruised
225 g (8 oz/1 cup) long grain rice, rinsed
salt

Rinse a heavy saucepan with water. Pour in the coconut milk, add the lemon grass and bring to a boil. Stir in the rice and return to a boil.

Stir rice; add salt to taste. Cover pan and cook very gently for 12 minutes until rice is tender and liquid has been absorbed. Without lifting lid, remove pan from the heat and leave to stand for 30 minutes. Discard lemon grass. Stir rice with chopsticks or a fork to fluff up grains.

Serves 3-4 as a side dish.

RICE WITH PRAWNS AND CHICKEN

225 g (8 oz/1 cup) long grain white rice, rinsed
3 tablespoons vegetable oil
2 eggs, beaten
1 onion, chopped
2 fresh red chillies, cored, deseeded and chopped
2 cloves garlic, crushed
1 teaspoon shrimp paste
175 g (6 oz) boneless, skinless chicken breast, cut into thin strips
115 g (4 oz) raw, unpeeled large prawns (jumbo shrimp), peeled and deveined
2 tablespoons dark soy sauce
1 tablespoon light brown sugar
2 spring onions (scallions), including some green, sliced diagonally

Bring rice to a boil in 500 ml (18 fl oz/2¼ cups) water. Stir, cover pan and simmer over low heat for 12 minutes until rice is tender and water is absorbed. Without lifting lid, remove pan from heat and leave for 15 minutes. Uncover and stir. Spread on an oiled tray and leave for 30-60 minutes. Heat 1 tablespoon oil in a wok. Add eggs to make an omelette. When cool, roll up and slice. Mix onions, chillies, garlic and shrimp paste to a paste in a blender. Heat remaining oil in wok over medium-high heat. Add paste and cook for 30 seconds.

Increase heat to high. Add chicken and stir-fry for 2-3 minutes until opaque. Add prawns (shrimp) and stir-fry for 1-1½ minutes until just pink. Transfer chicken and prawns (shrimp) to paper towels. Lower heat to medium; add rice and stir for 1-2 minutes. Cover and cook for 3 minutes, stirring twice. Add soy sauce, sugar and spring onions (scallions). Stir-fry for 1 minutes. Return chicken and prawns (shrimp) to wok. Add egg strips and cook over high heat for 2-3 minutes.

Serves 4.

RICE, PRAWNS & BEAN CURD

175 g (6 oz/¾ cup) long-grain white rice
3 tablespoons vegetable oil
3 cloves garlic, chopped
1 small onion, chopped
115 g (4 oz) bean curd, drained and cut into about
  1 cm (½ in) cubes
2 small fresh red chillies, deseeded and finely
  chopped
1 tablespoon fish sauce
175 g (6 oz) peeled prawns (shrimp)
1 shallot, thinly sliced
Prawns (shrimp) in their shells and fresh coriander
  (cilantro) leaves, to garnish

Cook rice, see page 8-9. In a wok, heat oil, add garlic and onion and cook, stirring occasionally, for 3-4 minutes until lightly browned. Add bean curd and fry for about 3 minutes until browned. Add chillies and stir-fry briefly. Stir in fish sauce and rice for 2-3 minutes, then stir in prawns (shrimp).

Add shallot, stir quickly to mix, then transfer to a warmed serving plate. Garnish with chilli flower and prawns (shrimp) in their shells and scatter coriander (cilantro) leaves over rice mixture.

Serves 4.

SEAFOOD FRIED RICE

225 g (8 oz/1 cup) long-grain rice
3 tablespoons vegetable oil
1 clove garlic, chopped
2 shallots, chopped
115 g (4 oz) small cooked peeled prawns (shrimp)
115 g (4 oz/½ cup) crabmeat, flaked
salt and freshly ground black pepper
2-3 eggs, beaten
2 tablespoons Thai fish or soy sauce
chopped spring onions (scallions), to garnish

The day before, cook the rice as on pages 8-9, then refrigerate it, so that it is cold and dry when required.

Heat about 1 tablespoon oil in a wok or frying-pan and stir-fry the garlic and shallots for about 30 seconds, then add the prawns (shrimp) and crab meat with salt and pepper. Stir-fry for 2-3 minutes, remove from pan and set aside.

Heat remaining oil in the pan and lightly scramble beaten eggs. When just beginning to set hard, add the rice and stir-fry mixture for 2-3 minutes. Add prawns (shrimp) and crabmeat with the fish or soy sauce and blend well. Garnish with chopped spring onions (scallions) and serve at once.

Serves 4.

VEGETABLE DISHES

VEGETABLES IN SPICY SAUCE

2-3 tablespoons vegetable oil
1 cake bean curd, cut into small cubes
½ teaspoon finely chopped garlic
2 shallots, sliced
1 tablespoon curry powder
2 tablespoons soy sauce
1 tablespoon chopped lemon grass
1 tablespoon chopped fresh root ginger
1 teaspoon chilli sauce (optional)
250 ml (9 fl oz/1 cup) coconut milk
½ teaspoon salt
1 tablespoon sugar
2 small carrots and 1 onion, sliced
115-175 g (4-6 oz) cauliflower flowerets
225 g (8 oz) green beans, trimmed and cut in half
2 firm tomatoes, cut into wedges

Heat oil in a wok or large fry-pan (skillet) and fry the bean curd until well browned on all sides. Remove and drain. Stir-fry the garlic and shallots in the same oil for about 1 minute, then add curry powder, soy sauce, lemon grass, ginger and chilli sauce, if using, and continue cooking for a further 1 minute. Add the coconut milk, salt and sugar and bring to the boil.

Add the carrots, onion, cauliflower, beans and bean curd and stir-fry for 3-4 minutes, then add the tomatoes. Blend well and cook for a further 2 minutes. Serve at once.

Serves 4-6

Variation: For non-vegetarians, either Thai fish sauce or oyster sauce can be used instead of soy sauce for this dish.

FRIED FRENCH BEANS

2 tablespoons vegetable oil
1 clove garlic, chopped
1 small onion, sliced
450 g (1 lb) French (green) beans, topped, tailed, and cut in half
about 2 tablespoons stock or water
2-3 small red chillies, deseeded and shredded
2 firm tomatoes, cut into wedges
salt and freshly ground black pepper
½ teaspoon sugar
chopped fresh coriander (cilantro), to garnish (optional)

Heat oil in a wok or frying-pan (skillet) and stir-fry the garlic and onion for about 1 minute.

Add the French (green) beans and stir-fry for 2-3 minutes, adding a little stock or water if the beans seem to be too dry.

Add chillies and tomatoes, and stir-fry for a further 1 minute, then add salt, pepper and sugar and blend well. Serve the beans hot or cold, garnished with chopped coriander (cilantro), if wished.

Serves 4.

STIR-FRIED MANGE TOUT

2 tablespoons vegetable oil
3 cloves garlic, finely chopped
115 g (4 oz) lean pork, very finely chopped
450 g (1 lb) mange tout (snow peas)
½ teaspoon crushed palm sugar
1 tablespoon fish sauce
55 g (2 oz) cooked peeled prawns (shrimp), chopped
freshly ground black pepper

In a wok, heat oil over a medium heat, add garlic and fry until lightly coloured. Add pork and stir-fry for 2-3 minutes.

Add mange tout (snow peas) and stir-fry for about 3 minutes until cooked but still crisp.

Stir in sugar, fish sauce, prawns (shrimp) and black pepper. Heat briefly and serve.

Serves 4-6.

STIR-FRIED SUGAR SNAP PEAS

225 g (8 oz) sugar snap peas
1½ tablespoons vegetable oil
6 cloves garlic with skins on, lightly bruised
115 g (4 oz) raw peeled medium prawns (shrimp)
2 tablespoons light soy sauce
1½ tablespoons oyster sauce
1 teaspoon rice wine
115 ml (4 fl oz/½ cup) fish stock or water blended with 1 teaspoon cornflour (cornstarch)
freshly ground black pepper (optional)

Bring a large saucepan of water to a boil. Quickly add sugar snap peas and immediately return to a boil. Boil for 5 seconds then drain thoroughly.

Heat oil in a wok or large frying pan (skillet) over high heat. Add garlic and stir-fry or a few seconds. Add prawns (shrimp) and stir-fry until colour changes to pink. Add peas, soy sauce, oyster sauce and rice wine. Stir-fry for 30 seconds.

Stir in cornflour (cornstarch) mixture and bring to a boil, stirring. Add black pepper, if liked, and serve.

Serves 4.

GARLIC AUBERGINES

450 g (1 lb) aubergines (eggplant)
4 tablespoons salt
1 tablespoon sunflower oil
2 cloves garlic, thinly sliced
3 tablespoons dark soy sauce
5 tablespoons rice wine
1 tablespoon yellow bean sauce
freshly ground black pepper
4 spring onions (scallions), finely chopped
shredded and sliced spring onions (scallions), to
  garnish

Halve aubergines (eggplant) lengthwise.
Halve again and cut into 1 cm (½ in) thick
pieces.

Layer aubergines (eggplant) in a bowl with
the salt and leave for 30 minutes. Rinse well
and dry on kitchen paper. Heat the oil in a
non-stick or well seasoned wok and stir-fry
aubergines (eggplant) and garlic for 2-3
minutes until lightly browned.

Add all remaining ingredients except the
spring onions (scallions). Bring to the boil,
reduce heat and simmer for 5 minutes until
softened. Stir in chopped spring onions
(scallions), garnish with shredded and sliced
spring onions (scallions) and serve. Ideal
accompaniment for Stir-fried Sesame Lamb,
page 70.

Serves 4.

AUBERGINES IN SPICY SAUCE

450 g (1 lb) aubergines (eggplants), cut into small
  strips, rather like potato chips
2-3 tablespoons vegetable oil
1 clove garlic, chopped
2 shallots, finely chopped
salt and freshly ground black pepper
½ teaspoon sugar
2-3 small hot red chillies, deseeded and chopped
2 tomatoes, cut into wedges
1 tablespoon soy sauce
1 teaspoon chilli sauce
1 tablespoon rice vinegar
about 115 ml (4 fl oz/½ cup) vegetarian stock
2 teaspoons cornflour (cornstarch)
½ teaspoon sesame oil
fresh coriander (cilantro) sprigs, to garnish

Stir-fry the aubergines (eggplants) in a dry
wok or frying pan for 3-4 minutes until soft
and a small amount of natural juice has
appeared. Remove and set aside. Heat the oil
and stir-fry garlic and shallots for about 30
seconds. Add the aubergines (eggplants),
salt, pepper, sugar and chillies and stir-fry for
2-3 minutes.

Add the tomatoes, soy sauce, chilli sauce,
vinegar and stock, blend well and bring to
the boil. Reduce heat and simmer for 3-4
minutes. Mix cornflour (cornstarch) with 1
tablespoon water and stir into sauce to
thicken it. Blend in sesame oil, garnish and
serve at once.

Serves 4.

Variation: For non-vegetarians, Thai fish
sauce or shrimp paste can be used instead of
soy sauce.

MUSHROOMS & BEANSPROUTS

2 tablespoons vegetable oil
2 fresh red chillies, deseeded and thinly sliced
2 cloves garlic, chopped
225 g (8 oz) shiitake mushrooms, sliced
115 g (4 oz/1 cup) beansprouts
115 g (4 oz) cooked peeled prawns (shrimp)
2 tablespoons lime juice
2 red shallots, sliced into rings
1 tablespoon Thai fish sauce
½ teaspoon crushed palm sugar
1 tablespoon ground browned rice (see page 8-9)
6 fresh coriander (cilantro) sprigs, stalks and leaves
  finely chopped
10 fresh Thai mint leaves, shredded
fresh Thai mint leaves, to garnish

In a wok, heat oil, add chillies and garlic and cook, stirring occasionally, for 2-3 minutes. Add mushrooms and stir-fry for 2-3 minutes.

Add beansprouts and prawns (shrimp), stir-fry for 1 minute, then stir in lime juice, shallots, fish sauce and sugar. When hot, remove from heat and stir in rice, coriander (cilantro) and mint. Serve garnished with mint leaves.

Serves 4.

BROCCOLI WITH SHRIMPS

3 tablespoons peanut oil
4 cloves garlic, finely chopped
1 fresh red chilli, deseeded and thinly sliced
450 g (1 lb) trimmed broccoli, cut diagonally into
  2.5 cm (1 in) slices
115 g (4 oz) cooked peeled shrimps
1 tablespoon Thai fish sauce
½ teaspoon crushed palm sugar

In a wok, heat oil, add garlic and fry, stirring occasionally, until just beginning to colour. Add chilli and cook for 2 minutes.

Quickly stir in broccoli. Stir-fry for 3 minutes. Reduce heat, cover wok and cook for 4-5 minutes until broccoli is cooked but still crisp.

Remove lid, stir in shrimps, fish sauce and sugar. Serve garnished with chilli flowers.

Serves 4.

TOSSED GREENS

2 tablespoons peanut oil
225 g (8 oz) chicken breast meat, very finely chopped
6 cloves garlic, finely chopped
700 g (1½ lb) spinach leaves, torn into large pieces if necessary
1½ tablespoons Thai fish sauce
freshly ground black pepper
1½ tablespoons dry-fried unsalted peanuts, chopped
thinly sliced fresh deseeded chilli, to garnish

In a wok, heat oil, add chicken and stir-fry for 2-3 minutes. Using a slotted spoon, transfer to kitchen paper; set aside.

Add garlic to wok and fry until just coloured. Using slotted spoon, transfer half to absorbent kitchen paper; set aside. Increase heat beneath wok so oil is lightly smoking. Quickly add all spinach, stir briefly to coat with oil and garlic.

Scatter chicken over, sprinkle with fish sauce and pepper. Reduce heat, cover wok and simmer for 2-3 minutes. Scatter over peanuts and reserved garlic and garnish with sliced chilli. Serve immediately.

Serves 4.

COURGETTES WITH GINGER

2 tablespoons vegetable oil
small piece fresh root ginger, sliced
1 teaspoon finely chopped garlic
450 g (1 lb) courgettes (zucchini), peeled and cut into small wedges
1 small carrot, sliced
2-3 tablespoons stock or water
55 g (2 oz) straw mushrooms, halved lengthwise
1 tomato, sliced
2 spring onions (scallions), cut into short lengths
salt and freshly ground black pepper
½ teaspoon sugar
1 tablespoon Thai fish sauce

Heat oil in a wok or frying pan and stir-fry ginger and garlic for about 30 seconds until fragrant. Add the courgettes (zucchini) and carrot and stir-fry for about 2 minutes, then add the stock or water to create steam, and continue stirring another 1-2 minutes.

Add straw mushrooms, tomato and spring onions (scallions) with salt, pepper and sugar, blend well and cook for a further 1-2 minutes. Sprinkle with fish sauce and serve at once.

Serves 4.

Variation: Other fresh delicate vegetables, such as asparagus, mange tout (snow peas), green peppers (capsicums) or cucumber can be cooked in the same way.

SPICY CAULIFLOWER

SPICED GRILLED SQUASH

55 g (2 oz/¼ cup) whole almonds
1 large cauliflower, divided into flowerets
55 g (2 oz/4 tablespoons) butter
1 onion, finely chopped
½ teaspoon chilli powder
½ teaspoon turmeric
3-4 tablespoons lemon juice
55 g (2 oz/½ cup) dried breadcrumbs
salt and freshly ground black pepper
lime wedges and fresh parsley sprigs, to garnish

Heat the wok until hot. Add the almonds and stir-fry over a moderate heat until browned on all sides. Remove to a plate. When cool, chop almonds coarsely.

Half-fill the wok with water and over high heat bring to the boil. Add the cauliflower pieces and simmer for 2 minutes. Drain and rinse; set aside. Wipe wok dry and return to heat. Add butter to wok and swirl until melted. Add the onion, chilli powder and turmeric and stir-fry for 2-3 minutes until softened.

Add the blanched cauliflower pieces and lemon juice and stir-fry for 3-4 minutes until tender but still crisp. Add the breadcrumbs and chopped almonds and toss until cauliflower pieces are well coated. Season with salt and pepper. Turn into a serving dish and serve hot, garnished with lime wedges and parsley.

Serves 4-6.

2 small butternut squash, quartered and deseeded
2 cloves garlic, finely chopped
2 teaspoons ground cumin
2-3 tablespoons vegetable oil
½ lime
salt and freshly ground black pepper

Using a small, sharp knife make shallow criss-cross cuts in the flesh of each squash quarter.

In a bowl, mix together garlic, cumin, oil, a good squeeze of lime juice, and salt and pepper to taste. Brush over flesh side of each piece of squash, working it well into the cuts.

Preheat barbecue or grill (broiler). Cook squash quarters for 10-15 minutes until lightly browned and flesh is tender. Brush occasionally with any remaining cumin mixture.

Serves 4 as a side dish.

CHOI SUM WITH BEAN CURD

2 tablespoons vegetable oil
225 g (8 oz) Chinese flowering cabbage, washed and
  drained
85 g (3 oz) fermented bean curd
1 teaspoon toasted sesame seeds

SPINACH WITH SESAME

1½ tablespoons oyster sauce
450 g (1 lb) young spinach leaves
1½ tablespoons vegetable oil
2 cloves garlic, thinly sliced
1 teaspoon sesame oil
toasted sesame seeds, to garnish

Mix oyster sauce with 1 tablespoon boiling water. Set aside. Bring a large saucepan of water to a boil. Quickly add spinach and return to a boil for 30 seconds. Drain very well.

In a wok, heat oil and fry cabbage for 1 minute. Using a slotted spoon, remove from wok, drain on absorbent kitchen paper then chop and arrange on a plate. Pour over bean curd and sprinkle with sesame seeds.

Serves 4.

Note: Other Chinese cabbages could be substituted if the flowering variety is not available.

Transfer spinach to a warm serving dish. Trickle oyster sauce mixture over spinach. Keep warm.

Meanwhile, in a wok or small frying pan (skillet) heat oil. Add garlic and fry until just turning golden. Scatter over spinach and trickle a little sesame oil over. Scatter sesame seeds on top and serve.

Serves 4 as a side dish.

SPICED CABBAGE

14 black peppercorns
2 tablespoons coconut cream, see page 8-9
2 shallots, chopped
115 g (4 oz) lean pork, very finely chopped
about 450 g (1 lb) white cabbage, finely sliced
300 ml (10 fl oz/1¼ cups) coconut milk
1 tablespoon Thai fish sauce
1 fresh red chilli, deseeded and very finely chopped

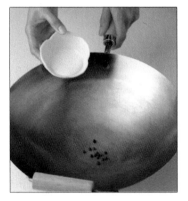

In a wok, heat peppercorns for about 3 minutes until aroma changes. Stir in coconut cream, heat for 2-3 minutes, then stir in shallots.

Stir-fry for a further 2-3 minutes, then stir in pork and cabbage. Cook, stirring occasionally, for 3 minutes, then add coconut milk and bring just to the boil. Cover and simmer for 5 minutes.

Uncover and cook for about 10 minutes until cabbage is tender but retains some bite. Stir in fish sauce. Serve sprinkled with chilli.

Serves 4-5.

SESAME GARLIC VEGETABLES

225 g (8 oz) broccoli
1 large green pepper (capsicum)
225 g (8 oz) courgettes (zucchini)
225 g (8 oz) asparagus
2 cloves garlic, thinly sliced
2 teaspoons sesame oil
1 tablespoon sesame seeds
soy sauce, to serve

Slice the broccoli into small flowerets. Slice courgettes (zucchini) into 2.5 cm (1 in) pieces and halve. Cut pepper (capsicum) into 8. Trim away tough ends from asparagus and slice into 5 cm (2 in) pieces. Place vegetables in a colander and rinse well.

Bring a wok or large saucepan of water to the boil. Arrange vegetables on a layer of baking parchment in a steamer and place over the water. Sprinkle with sliced garlic and sesame oil. Cover and steam for 10 minutes.

Remove vegetables from steamer and place on warmed serving plates. Sprinkle with sesame seeds and serve with soy sauce, for dipping.

Serves 4.

OKRA IN SPICE SAUCE

2 tablespoons dried shrimps
3 fresh red chillies, cored, deseeded and chopped
4 cloves garlic, chopped
1½ teaspoons shrimp paste
3 shallots, chopped
3 tablespoons vegetable oil
225 g (8 oz) fresh okra, conical caps and tips cut off
1 tablespoon lime juice
freshly ground black pepper

Soak dried shrimps in hot water for 10 minutes. Drain and put in a blender. Add chillies, garlic, shrimp paste and shallots. Mix to a paste, adding a little water if necessary.

In a wok or frying pan (skillet), heat oil over medium-high heat. Add okra and stir for about 5 minutes. Remove with a slotted spoon and set aside.

Add spice paste to pan and stir for 1 minute. Lower heat and return okra to pan with the lime juice, 4 tablespoons water and plenty of black pepper. Bring to a simmer then cook gently, stirring occasionally, for 5 minutes or until okra is tender.

Serves 3-4 as a side dish.

VEGETABLE STIR-FRY

2 tablespoons groundnut oil
2 fresh red chillies, cored, deseeded and finely chopped
2.5 cm (1 in) piece fresh root ginger, grated
2 cloves garlic, crushed
115 g (4 oz) each carrots, cut into matchsticks, French (green) beans, broccoli florets and baby sweetcorn, halved
1 red pepper (capsicum), cut into fine strips
2 small pak choi, very coarsely chopped
4 spring onions (scallions), including some green, sliced
1 tablespoon hot curry paste
300 ml (10 fl oz/1¼ cups) coconut milk
2 tablespoons Satay Sauce (see page 76)
2 tablespoons soy sauce
1 teaspoon light brown sugar
4 tablespoons chopped fresh coriander (cilantro)
whole roasted peanuts, to garnish

In a wok or sauté pan, heat oil. Add chillies, ginger and garlic. Stir-fry for 1 minute. Add carrot, French beans, broccoli, sweetcorn, pepper (capsicum). Over high heat, stir-fry for 3-4 minutes. Stir in pak choi, spring onions (scallions) and curry paste and stir-fry for 1-2 minutes longer.

Stir in coconut milk, satay sauce, soy sauce and sugar. Bring to boil then simmer 1-2 minutes until vegetables are just tender. Add coriander (cilantro) then serve garnished with peanuts.

Serves 4-6.

SALADS AND ACCOMPANIMENTS

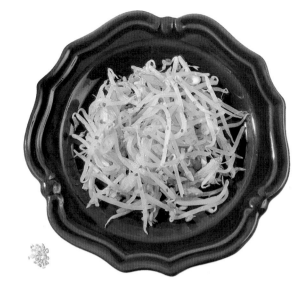

PRAWN SALAD WITH MINT

BEAN SPROUT SALAD

16-20 raw large prawns (shrimp), peeled and deveined
juice 2 limes
2 teaspoons vegetable oil
2 teaspoons crushed palm sugar
2 tablespoons tamarind water, see page 8-9
1 tablespoon fish sauce
2 teaspoons Thai red curry paste
2 stalks lemon grass, very finely chopped
4 tablespoons coconut cream, see page 8-9
10 fresh Thai mint leaves, shredded
5 kaffir lime leaves, shredded
1 small crisp lettuce, divided into leaves
1 small cucumber, thinly sliced
fresh Thai mint leaves, to garnish

salt
575 (1¼ lb) bean sprouts
1 tablespoon sesame seeds
1 fresh red chilli, cored, deseeded and chopped
2 cloves garlic, finely chopped
2 tablespoons sesame oil
4 spring onions (scallion) including the green, very thinly sliced

Bring a large saucepan of salted water to a boil. Add the bean sprouts all at once. Cover the pan and quickly return to a boil. Uncover the pan and boil for 30 seconds.

Put prawns (shrimp) in a bowl, pour over lime juice and leave for 30 minutes. Remove prawns (shrimp), allowing excess liquid to drain into bowl; reserve liquid. Heat oil in a wok, add prawns (shrimp) and stir-fry for 2-3 minutes until just cooked – marinating in lime juice partially cooks them.

Tip bean sprouts into a colander and rinse under running cold water. Press bean sprouts gently to squeeze out surplus water. Transfer bean sprouts to a bowl. Heat a small heavy frying pan (skillet). Add sesame seeds and dry-fry, stirring, until fragrant and lightly browned. Add to bean sprouts.

Meanwhile, stir sugar, tamarind water, fish sauce, curry paste, lemon grass, coconut cream, mint and lime leaves into reserved lime liquid. Stir in cooked prawns. Set aside until cold. Make a bed of lettuce on a serving plate, place on a layer cucumber slices. Spoon prawns (shrimp) and dressing on top. Garnish with mint leaves.

Serves 3-4.

Add chilli, garlic, sesame oil and spring onions (scallions) to a bowl with bean sprouts. Toss to mix ingredients thoroughly.

Serves 4 as a side dish.

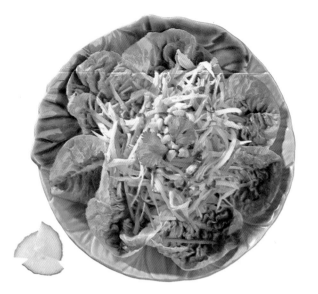

SPICY CHICKEN SALAD

225-300 g (8-10 oz) boneless cooked chicken meat, shredded
½ cucumber, thinly shredded
1 carrot and 1 small onion, thinly shredded
salt and freshly ground black pepper
few lettuce leaves
2 small red chillies, deseeded and shredded
1 tablespoon roasted peanuts, crushed
fresh coriander (cilantro) sprigs, to garnish
Dressing:
1 clove garlic, chopped
1 teaspoon chopped fresh root ginger
1-2 small red or green chillies, chopped
1 tablespoon sugar
2 tablespoons each Thai fish sauce and lime juice
1 tablespoon sesame oil

In a bowl, mix together chicken, cucumber, carrot and onion and season with salt and pepper. Arrange a bed of lettuce leaves on a serving dish or plate and spoon the chicken mixture on top.

Using a pestle and mortar, pound the garlic, ginger, chillies and sugar to a fine paste, then blend the paste with the rest of the dressing ingredients. Pour the dressing all over the salad just before serving, and garnish with the chillies, peanuts and coriander (cilantro) sprigs.

Serves 4-6.

Note: Do not toss and mix the salad with the dressing until ready to serve.

PRAWN & CUCUMBER SALAD

1 teaspoon chilli oil
1 teaspoon Szechuan peppercorns, toasted and ground
pinch of salt
1 tablespoon white rice vinegar
1 teaspoon caster sugar
350 g (12 oz) cooked, peeled prawns (shrimp), thawed and dried, if frozen
¼ cucumber
1 tablespoon sesame seeds
½ head Chinese leaves, shredded
fresh red chilli strips and lemon wedges, to garnish

In a large bowl, mix together the oil, peppercorns, salt, vinegar and sugar.

Add the prawns (shrimp) and mix well. Cover and chill for 30 minutes. Thinly slice the cucumber and slice each piece into thin strips. Pat dry with kitchen paper and mix into prawns (shrimp) with sesame seeds.

Arrange the Chinese leaves on 4 serving plates and top with the prawn (shrimp) mixture. Garnish with chilli strips and lemon wedges and serve immediately.

Serves 4.

CHICKEN & MINT SALAD

1 stalk lemon grass, finely chopped
2-3 fresh red chillies, deseeded and finely chopped
3 tablespoons lime juice
1 tablespoon Thai fish sauce
2 teaspoons crushed palm sugar
1½ tablespoons vegetable oil
450 g (1 lb) skinless chicken breast meat, very finely chopped
15 fresh Thai mint leaves, shredded
lettuce leaves, to serve

In a bowl, mix together lemon grass, chillies, lime juice, fish sauce and sugar; set aside.

In a wok, heat oil, stir in chicken and cook over a fairly high heat, stirring, for about 1½ minutes until cooked thoroughly. Using a slotted spoon, quickly transfer to absorbent kitchen paper to drain, then add to bowl.

Add mint and toss lightly. Serve on a bed of lettuce leaves, garnished with mint sprig and chilli flowers.

Serves 4.

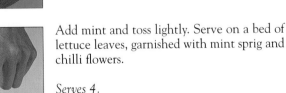

CHICKEN & WATERCRESS SALAD

2 cloves garlic, finely chopped
3 cm (1¼ in) piece galangal, finely chopped
1 tablespoon fish sauce
3 tablespoons lime juice
1 teaspoon crushed palm sugar
2 tablespoons peanut oil
225 g (8 oz) chicken breast meat, finely chopped
about 25 dried shrimps
1 bunch watercress, about 115 g (4 oz), coarse stalks removed
3 tablespoons chopped dry-roasted peanuts
2 fresh red chillies, deseeded and cut into fine strips

Using a pestle and mortar, pound together garlic and galangal. Mix in fish sauce, lime juice and sugar; set aside. In a wok, heat oil, add chicken and stir-fry for about 3 minutes until cooked through. Using a slotted spoon, transfer to kitchen paper to drain. Put into a serving bowl and set aside.

Chop half dried shrimps and add to bowl. Mix in watercress, peanuts and half of chillies. Pour over garlic mixture and toss to mix. Sprinkle with remaining chillies and shrimps.

Serves 3-4.

BEEF & ORANGE SALAD

1 tablespoon groundnut (peanut) oil
4 × 115 g (4 oz) lean beef fillet steaks, trimmed and
    tenderized
3 tablespoons dark soy sauce
3 tablespoons dry sherry
1 teaspoon ground cinnamon
1 tablespoon brown sugar
freshly ground black pepper
115 g (4 oz) canned water chestnuts, rinsed and
    sliced
175 g (6 oz) fresh young spinach leaves
115 g (4 oz) spring onions (scallions), shredded
2 oranges, peeled and segmented
strips of orange rind, to garnish

Heat oil in a non-stick or well seasoned wok
and fry beef steaks for 2 minutes on each
side. Drain on kitchen paper and wipe out
wok. Mix together soy sauce, dry sherry, cinnamon, brown sugar and pepper. Return
steaks to the wok, add water chestnuts and
pour over soy sauce mixture. Bring to the
boil, reduce heat and simmer for 5-6
minutes, turning steaks halfway through.

Arrange spinach leaves on serving plates and
top each with a steak, water chestnut and
sauce. Sprinkle with spring onions (scallions) and top with orange segments.
Garnish with strips of orange rind and serve
immediately.

Serves 4.

PORK & BAMBOO SHOOT SALAD

3 tablespoons vegetable oil
3 cloves garlic, chopped
1 small onion, thinly sliced
225 g (8 oz) lean pork, very finely chopped
1 egg, beaten
225 g (8 oz) can bamboo shoots, drained and cut
    into strips
1 tablespoon Thai fish sauce
1 teaspoon crushed palm sugar
3 tablespoons lime juice
freshly ground black pepper
lettuce leaves, to serve

In a wok, heat 2 tablespoons oil, add garlic
and onion and cook, stirring occasionally,
until lightly browned. Using a slotted spoon,
transfer to absorbent kitchen paper to drain;
set aside. Add pork to wok and stir-fry for
about 3 minutes until cooked through. Using
a slotted spoon, transfer to kitchen paper; set
aside. Using kitchen paper, wipe out wok.

Heat remaining oil, pour in egg to make a
thin layer and cook for 1-2 minutes until just
set. Turn egg over and cook for 1 minute
more. Remove egg from wok and roll up. Cut
across strips. In a bowl, toss together pork,
bamboo shoots and egg. In a small bowl, stir
together fish sauce, sugar, lime juice and
pepper. Pour over pork mixture and toss.
Serve on lettuce leaves and sprinkle with
garlic and onion.

Serves 3-4.

FRESH MINT SAMBAL

55 g (2 oz/2 cups) mint leaves
1 cm (½ in) piece of fresh root ginger, coarsely
  chopped
1 small onion, coarsely chopped
4 tablespoons lime juice
salt

Put mint, ginger, onion and lime juice in a
blender. Mix to a paste. Season with salt to
taste.

Transfer sambal to a small serving bowl.
Serve sambal with curries or Curry Puffs (see
page 21).

Makes about 225 ml (8 fl oz/1 cup).

HOT SAUCE

1 clove garlic, chopped
2 small red or green chillies, deseeded and chopped
1 teaspoon finely chopped fresh root ginger
1 tablespoon chilli sauce
2 sticks lemon grass, peeled and chopped
2 tablespoons vegetable oil
2 tablespoons soy sauce
1 tablespoon Thai fish sauce
2 tablespoons sugar
2 tablespoons lime juice with pulp
4-6 tablespoons chicken stock or water
2 tablespoons chopped fresh coriander leaves
1 tablespoon cornflour (cornstarch)

Using a pestle and mortar, pound the garlic,
chillies, ginger, chilli sauce and lemon grass
to a paste. Heat oil in a medium saucepan
and gently stir-fry the paste with soy sauce,
fish sauce, sugar, lime juice and stock or
water, then bring to the boil.

Blend in chopped coriander (cilantro). Mix
cornflour (cornstarch) with 2 tablespoons
water and stir the paste into the sauce to
thicken it. Remove from heat and serve.

Makes about 350 ml (12 fl oz/1½ cups).

Note: This highly spiced sauce goes well
with all sorts of meat or fish dishes - it can
form the base for curry sauce, or it can be
served as a dip.

MANGO CHUTNEY

2 kg (4 lb) unripe mangoes, peeled and cubed
2 limes, sliced into semi-circles
3 fresh red chillies, cored, deseeded and finely chopped
750 ml (25 fl oz/3 cups/2 tablespoons) white wine
　vinegar
1 tablespoon ground toasted cardamom seeds
1 teaspoon ground toasted cumin seeds
1 teaspoon ground turmeric
1½ teaspoons salt
450 g (1 lb/2 cups) light brown sugar

Put mangoes, limes, chillies and vinegar into a non-reactive pan. Bring to a boil then lower heat and simmer, uncovered, for 10-15 minutes until mangoes are just tender.

Add spices, salt and sugar. Stir until sugar has dissolved then increase heat and bring to a boil. Lower heat again and simmer, uncovered, for 50-60 minutes, stirring occasionally, until most of the liquid has evaporated and the chutney is quite thick.

Ladle chutney into hot, very clean jars. Cover top of each jar of chutney with a disc of waxed paper, waxed side down. Close jars with non-reactive lids. Leave chutney for 1 month before using.

Makes 1.5 kg (3 lb).

DIPPING SAUCE & SPICY SAUCE

DIPPING SAUCE
1 garlic clove, crushed
salt
4 tablespoons light soy sauce
2½ tablespoons lime juice
1 tablespoon very finely sliced spring onion (scallion)
1 teaspoon light brown sugar
1 or 2 drops of chilli sauce

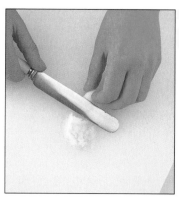

Mash the garlic clove with a very small pinch of salt. In a small dish, put garlic, soy sauce, lime juice, spring onion (scallion) and sugar. Add chilli sauce to taste. Stir before serving.

Serves 4.

SPICY SAUCE
4 dried red chillies, cored, deseeded and chopped
6 tablespoons groundnut oil
4 shallots, finely chopped
8 cloves garlic, finely chopped
150 g (5 oz) ripe tomato, coarsely chopped
1 teaspoon ground coriander seeds
1 teaspoon ground cumin seeds
1 teaspoon light brown sugar

In a small bowl, soak chillies in 3 tablespoons hot water for 15 minutes. Drain and reserve. Heat oil in a frying pan (skillet) over medium-low heat. Add shallots and fry until softened.

Add garlic, tomato, coriander seeds, cumin seeds and sugar to pan. Bring to a boil then simmer for 3-4 minutes. Pour into a fine sieve (strainer) placed over a bowl. Press through as much of the contents of sieve (strainer) as possible. Cover and keep in a cool place until required.

Serves 6.

SPICY FISH SAUCE

QUICK MIXED PICKLE

2 cloves garlic
2 small red or green chillies, deseeded and chopped
1 tablespoon sugar
2 tablespoons lime juice
2 tablespoons Thai fish sauce

2 fresh red chillies, cored, deseeded and chopped
7 shallots, 5 chopped, 2 left whole
6 cloves garlic, 3 chopped, 3 left whole
4 cm (1½ in) piece fresh root ginger, grated
175 g (6 oz) cauliflower flowerets
4 small carrots, cut into fine sticks
175 g (6 oz) unpeeled cucumber, cut into fine sticks
3 tablespoons vegetable oil
1 tablespoon curry powder
½ teaspoon each black mustard seeds and ground
  turmeric
2 teaspoons light brown sugar
4 tablespoons rice vinegar
salt
1 tablespoon sesame oil
1 tablespoon toasted sesame seeds

Using a pestle and mortar, pound garlic and chillies until finely ground. If you do not have a pestle and mortar, just finely mince the garlic and chillies.

Put chillies, chopped shallots and chopped garlic and ¾ ginger in a blender. Add 1 tablespoon water and mix to a paste. Bring a large saucepan of water to a boil. Add cauliflower and carrots. Quickly return to a boil. After 30 seconds add cucumber and boil for about 3 seconds. Tip into a colander and rinse under running cold water.

Place mixture in a bowl and add sugar, lime juice, fish sauce and 2-3 tablespoons water. Blend well. Serve in small dipping saucers.

Serves 4.

Note: This sauce is known as nuoc cham. You can make a large quantity of the base for later use by boiling the lime juice, fish sauce and water with sugar in a pan. It will keep for months in a tightly sealed jar or bottle in the refrigerator. Add freshly minced garlic and chillies for serving.

Heat oil in a large saucepan. Add spice paste and fry for 1 minute. Add whole shallots and whole garlic and remaining ginger. Stir-fry for 30 seconds. Reduce heat to medium low. Stir in curry powder, mustard seeds, turmeric and sugar. Add vinegar, blanched vegetables and 1½ tablespoons salt. Bring to a boil. Remove from heat and stir in sesame oil and sesame seeds. Cool then ladle into a warm jar. Cover with non-reactive lid. Refrigerate when cold.

Makes 900 ml (30 fl oz/4 cups).

DESSERTS

FRUIT SALAD

115 g (4 oz/½ cup) rock candy or crystal sugar
about 350 g (12 fl oz/1½ cups) boiling water
½ small watermelon or a whole honeydew melon
4-5 different fruits (fresh or canned), such as
  pineapple, grapes, lychees, rambutan, banana,
  papaya, mango or kiwi fruit
crushed ice cubes

Make a syrup by dissolving the rock candy in the boiling water, then leave to cool.

Slice about 7.5 cm (3 in) off the top of melon, scoop out flesh, discarding seeds, and cut flesh into small chunks. Prepare all the other fruits by cutting them into small chunks the same size as the melon chunks.

Fill melon shell with the fruit and syrup. Cover with plastic wrap and chill in the refrigerator for at least 2-3 hours. Serve on a bed of crushed ice.

Serves 4-6.

Note: If using canned fruit with syrup or natural juice, you can use this instead of making syrup for the dessert.

LYCHEE SORBET

450 g (1 lb) fresh lychees in their shells or 175 g
  (6 oz) canned lychees
about 115 ml (4 fl oz/½ cup) syrup, see opposite
mint sprigs, to decorate

Peel fresh lychees and stone them. Place the lychees in a food processor or blender with the syrup and process to a smooth purée.

Pour the purée into a freezerproof container and place in the freezer for about 2 hours until almost set.

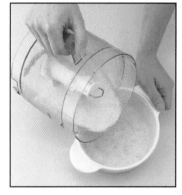

Break up the iced mixture and whip until smooth. Return mixture to the freezer for 30-45 minutes to set until solid. Serve the sorbet decorated with mint leaves.

Serves 4-6.

Variation: 2 teaspoons grated root ginger can be added to the sorbet mixture before blending, if wished.

GREEN TEA FRUIT SALAD

4 teaspoons jasmine tea leaves
2 tablespoons dry sherry
2 tablespoons caster sugar
1 lime
2 kiwi fruit
225 g (8 oz) fresh lychees
¼ honeydew melon
115 g (4 oz) seedless green grapes
lime slices, to decorate

Place tea leaves in a small bowl or jug and pour over 300 ml (10 fl oz/1¼ cups) boiling water. Leave to steep for 5 minutes. Pour through a sieve (strainer) into a saucepan.

Stir in sherry and sugar. Using a vegetable peeler, pare the rind from the lime and add to the pan. Squeeze the juice from the lime and add to the juice to the pan. Bring to the boil, reduce heat and simmer for 5 minutes. Leave to cool, then discard lime rind.

Peel and thinly slice kiwi fruit. Peel, halve and stone the lychees. Peel melon and slice thinly. Arrange prepared fruits and grapes in small clusters on serving plates. Pour over cooled tea syrup, decorate and serve.

Serves 4.

PINEAPPLE WITH COCONUT

100 g (3½ oz) caster (superfine) sugar
3.75 cm (1½ in) piece fresh root ginger, grated
100 g (3½ oz/scant ½ cup) light brown sugar
12 thin slices fresh pineapple
3-4 tablespoons toasted coconut flakes

Put caster (superfine) sugar, ginger and light brown sugar in a heavy based saucepan. Stir in 375 ml (13 fl oz/1⅔ cups) water. Heat gently, stirring with a wooden spoon, until sugars have melted. Bring to a boil. Simmer until reduced by about ⅓.

Remove cores from slices of pineapple using a small sharp knife or a small biscuit (cookie) cutter. Strain syrup over pineapple rings and leave to cool. Cover and chill.

To serve, lay 2 pineapple rings on each plate. Spoon some of the syrup over and scatter the toasted coconut flakes on top.

Serves 6.

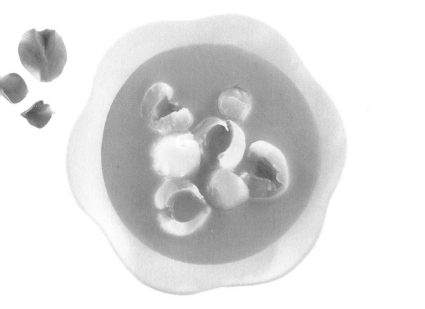

LYCHEES & COCONUT CUSTARD

3 egg yolks
3-4 tablespoons caster sugar
200 ml (7 fl oz/scant 1 cup) coconut milk
85 ml (3 fl oz/⅓ cup) coconut cream, see page 8-9
about 1 tablespoon triple distilled rose water
red food colouring
about 16 fresh lychees, peeled, halved and stones
  removed
rose petals, to decorate

In a bowl, whisk together egg yolks and sugar.

In a medium, preferably non-stick, saucepan, heat coconut milk to just below boiling point, then slowly stir into bowl. Return to pan and cook very gently, stirring with a wooden spoon, until custard coats the back of the spoon.

Remove from heat and stir in coconut cream, rose water to taste and sufficient red food colouring to colour pale pink. Leave until cold, stirring occasionally. Spoon a thin layer of rose-flavoured custard into 4 small serving bowls. Arrange lychees on custard. Decorate with rose petals. Serve remaining custard separately to pour over lychees.

Serves 4.

CARAMEL SESAME BANANAS

4 bananas
juice of 1 lemon
115 g (4 oz/½ cup) caster (superfine) sugar
2 tablespoons sesame seeds
mint sprigs and lemon slices, to decorate

Peel bananas and cut into 5 cm (2 in) pieces. Place in a bowl, pour over the lemon juice and stir well to coat.

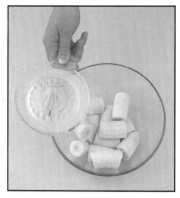

Place sugar and 4 tablespoons water in a saucepan and heat gently, stirring, until the sugar dissolves. Bring to the boil and cook for 5-6 minutes until the mixture caramelizes and turns golden brown. Drain bananas well and arrange on a layer of baking parchment.

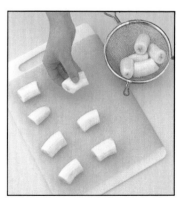

Drizzle the caramel over the bananas, working quickly as the caramel sets within a few seconds. Sprinkle with the sesame seeds. Allow to cool for 5 minutes, then carefully peel away from paper, decorate and serve.

Serves 4.

COCONUT CUSTARDS

1 pandan leaf (optional)
550 ml (20 fl oz/2½ cups) coconut milk
3 whole eggs
3 egg yolks
about 85 g (3 oz/⅓ cup) caster (superfine) sugar
115 ml (4 fl oz/½ cup) single (light) cream

Run the tines of a fork through the pandan leaf, if using. Tie in a knot. Pour coconut milk into a non-stick saucepan, add pandan leaf and bring to just below a simmer. Remove from heat, cover and leave for 20 minutes. Discard pandan leaf.

Preheat oven to 180C (350F/Gas 4). Reheat (or heat) coconut milk to a boil. In a bowl, whisk together eggs, egg yolk and sugar until evenly blended. Slowly pour in coconut milk, whisking constantly. Add cream.

Strain into jug and pour into 8 ramekin dishes. Set ramekins in a roasting tin (pan) and pour boiling water into a tin (pan) to come halfway up sides of ramekins. Cook in oven for 20-25 minutes until a skewer inserted in centre comes out clean. Remove ramekins from tin (pan) and leave to cool. Chill until required.

Serves 8.

SAGO PUDDING

450 ml (16 fl oz/2 cups) milk or water
175 g (6 oz/1 cup) sago, rinsed
350 ml (12 fl oz/1½ cups) coconut milk
55 ml (2 fl oz/¼ cup) single (light) cream
Syrup
150 g (5 oz/⅔ cup) palm sugar or brown sugar
small piece fresh root ginger or lemon grass
1 pandan leaf (optional)

In a saucepan, bring milk or water to a boil. Add sago, stir and simmer for 10-15 minutes, stirring occasionally, until tender. Cool slightly and spoon into individual glass dishes. Cool completely then refrigerate.

To make syrup, in a saucepan, gently heat sugar with 175 ml (6 fl oz/¾ cup) water and the ginger or lemon grass, and pandan leaf, if using, stirring with a wooden spoon until sugar has dissolved. Bring to a boil. Simmer for a few minutes until syrup thickens. Strain and leave to cool.

Mix together coconut milk and cream, then chill. To serve, pour creamy coconut milk around edges of sago puddings. Make a well in the centre of the puddings and pour in some of the syrup.

Serves 6.

STUFFED RAMBUTANS

1 small banana, chopped
grated rind and juice of 1 lime
16 rambutans
85 g (3 oz/½ cup) stoned dates, chopped
1 papaya, peeled, seeded and chopped
strips of lime rind, to decorate

Mix the banana with the lime rind and juice and set aside. Slice the top off rambutans, exposing the tip of the stone. Using a sharp, small-bladed knife, carefully slice down around the stone, loosening the flesh away from the stone.

Peel away the skin, and slice lengthwise through flesh at quarterly intervals. Gently pull down the flesh to expose the stone (pit) and carefully cut away the stone. The flesh should now resemble a four-petalled flower.

In a food processor or blender, blend banana and dates until smooth. Place a teaspoon of filling in the centre of each rambutan and bring up the sides to enclose the filling. Cover and chill for 30 minutes. Blend the papaya in a food processor or blender until smooth, pass through a sieve and spoon on to four serving plates. Top with rambutans, decorate with strips of lime rind and serve.

Serves 4.

FRUIT-FILLED WHITE CREPES

3 egg whites, lightly beaten
4 tablespoons cornflour (cornstarch)
1 teaspoon sunflower oil
mint sprigs, to decorate
Filling:
4 slices fresh pineapple, peeled, cored and chopped
2 kiwi fruit, peeled and quartered
½ mango, peeled, stoned (pitted) and sliced
½ papaya, peeled, deseeded and chopped
2 tablespoons dry sherry
1 tablespoon brown sugar
1 whole cinnamon stick, broken
2 star anise

Place all the filling ingredients in a non-stick or well seasoned wok and mix gently. Bring to the boil, reduce heat and simmer very gently for 10 minutes. Remove and discard cinnamon stick and star anise. Set aside. Meanwhile, make the crêpes. Put the egg whites and cornflour (cornstarch) in a jug and stir in 8 teaspoons water, mixing well to form a smooth paste.

Brush a non-stick or well seasoned crêpe pan with a little oil and heat. Pour in a quarter of the mixture, tilting the pan to cover the base. Cook for 1 minute on one side only, until set. Drain on kitchen paper, layer with baking parchment and keep warm whilst making the remaining 3 crêpes. Lay crêpes cooked-side up, fill with the fruit and fold crêpes over the filling. Decorate and serve.

Serves 4.

INDEX